Church Organization

A Manual for
Effective Local
Church Administration

James G. Pendorf
Helmer C. Lundquist

with a foreword by
The Rt. Rev. Alexander D. Stewart
Bishop of Western Massachusetts

Morehouse-Barlow
Wilton, Connecticut

Dedicated to our wives,

Sharon

and

Ruth

Foreword

Succinct, practical, constructive, time-saving, readable: such is the description of this book which will enable your vestry to *work smarter, not harder.* This book is written in plain English. It is not laden with jargon. It does not allow goal-setting to lead to parish paralysis, as so often happens; rather, it provides the pathway from planning to organizing to motivating and controlling.

With limited hours and energy available, your leadership will benefit from well developed and tested job descriptions, refining them of course for your own situation. How many organists have accepted a part-time position assuming they would be paid for vacation only to be told later, "Everyone knows that part-time people don't get paid for time off—our last organist didn't." How many paid holidays does the secretary receive? How would a new rector even know what the original agreement might have been?

Administration is not inherently evil but is a useful tool that enables us to serve the Lord and fulfill the mission entrusted to us. The word means literally "to minister to." Administration is the integrating concept. No stewardship program is effective without it. No education program endures without it. Effective social ministry to the community and persons in need requires organization. Even effective worship requires careful planning if what we offer to the Almighty is to be characterized by the grandeur and mystery characteristic of worship at its best.

Consider parish calling. The lay person hears an appeal for parish visitors by the vestry, or from the chancel steps or in the bulletin. He imagines himself as the only volunteer calling forever on the entire parish and echoes, "Not me, Lord." Suppose he heard instead, "Our Lord needs sixteen persons to visit in teams of two. That's eight teams. They will make two calls per week either on Thursday evening or Saturday afternoon for a three month period. That will result in 208 calls." Committed churchmen will respond, "YES," knowing for how long, how many, when, and with a partner. So a few minutes of planning results in 208 calls, bringing joyfully back to the fold many who have strayed. Our Lord challenged people personally, and with a specific task, "Arise and follow me and I will make you to be fishers of men." And the disciples responded. And later "the seventy returned with joy," St. Luke records.

Effective administration always introduces 'the multiplier effect' so that we

> distribute the load
> get the job done quickly
> get the job done completely
> reduce personal tension

Effective administration reduces—though it can never eliminate—the occasions when human beings collide, get hurt and leave the church, or if they remain, do so with residual bitterness and resentment. Their job, either as volunteers or as paid employees, was never clarified. The willing worker agrees to be in charge of the Church School and then discovers this involves producing a Christmas pageant, planning a picnic and representing the parish on the Education Committee of the Council of Churches. She envisioned curriculum planning and class supervision. The part-time sexton is engaged with instructions "to keep the church clean" at $50 per week. The sanctuary is spotless. But no one told him he was to wash parish hall windows, mow the lawn come spring, or change light bulbs for the weekday nursery program. So his grandmother is upset and on the miff tree when she hears he isn't doing his job.

Recent research on the Inactive and Apathetic Church Member by Dr. John Savage reveals that overwork frequently leads to total withdrawal from parish life. Even if the person remains overly active, Dr. Savage observes isolation of other family members from the church and resentment that " 'mother' or 'dad' spends all his time down there." What are they saying about family unity and the church?

When we *work smarter, not harder* we distribute the load among many parishioners, often finding hidden talents for the Lord's mission. And we don't give up because only one-third of the parish is involved. That's better than just the faithful few carrying the entire load.

Secure several copies so your vestry can read this book together. What a difference it could make as your parish, an outpost of the kingdom, becomes an effective cell of the everlasting Church, and the talents of many are employed in Christ's service.

The Rt. Rev. Alexander D. Stewart

Table of Contents

Preface

If you serve on the vestry, executive committee, or board of trustees of your local church and have ever wished for a job description which spelled out your task, then this little book should be just what you have always wanted. On page after page you will find examples of actual descriptions of various positions required for the effectively organized church. We ourselves have used these examples quite successfully for a number of years in different parochial settings. We have found written statements of accountability to be invaluable for clarifying the various functions and responsibilities of the many people involved in the total operation of a church.

To the best of our knowledge there is no other book currently available to which you can turn for ideas to develop your own written statement about the depth and scope of your particular assignment on the board of your congregation. You would have to start from scratch, or at best work with some hand-me-down notes from your predecessor. In any event, you might very well find yourself alone in your desire to have a carefully defined role. You could easily wind up feeling frustrated and misunderstood by your colleagues. This is all too often the case in so many churches, where regularly accepted good business practices are simply ignored or viewed with suspicion.

Now, with this manual, you can quickly come up with a description of your own position, and at the same time help the entire leadership of your board to specify exactly who is accountable for what. Our intent here is to make the process of defining functions and responsibilities so clear and comprehensible that your church board will be able to organize itself effectively with a minimum amount of difficulty. We have learned from our experiences in different congregations what needs to be emphasized and what needs to be avoided in designing and implementing a system of accountability for vestries and executive committees. We have done the tedious job of starting from the beginning without the benefit of a finished model from which to proceed, so there is no reason for you to have to do it all over again yourself. We hope you will be able to use our effort, to pick up where we have left off, and to develop your own effective church organization.

Before you get too involved with our chapters on position descriptions, do take the time to consider carefully the following two points. It is on these concepts that we base our entire work, so it is important that you understand them from the beginning.

First of all, in order for any organization to produce desired results, it is absolutely necessary to have an internal monitor or feedback system, which will provide for corrections and adjustments when required. Such a watchdog system is based on the experience that in any organization there are always deviations from expected norms which take special attention. It is never a question *if* something will go wrong; it is always a matter of what will be done *when* something goes wrong. We have certainly seen this to be the case in the Church, where "Murphy's Law" seems to apply so well: "In any given situation if something can go wrong, it will." To deal effectively with such situations, it is vital to have a monitoring system which will keep you informed of changes before they become too catastrophic to manage. In churches, we have found that such a system requires that facts be documented in writing, especially *who is accountable to whom for what and by when.* It is one matter to point out to a member of your board that an area of his responsibility mutually agreed upon in writing might need some additional attention, but quite another story to argue with someone who maintains that the proverbial "someone else" said they would take care of the situation, that "It's not my job!" By making the effort and taking the time to define functions and responsibilities to the point where they can be written down, you save time and trouble later on when things go wrong. Instead of first having to determine just who had previously agreed to do what work, which is not always the easiest thing to do, all that is necessary is to check your position descriptions and go immediately to the person designated in writing as the one responsible for the particular task.

Secondly, as you develop an effective local church administration by documenting in writing who is to do what, with enough copies available for everyone concerned, you must realize that written accountability is simply the means to an end and that a certain degree of flexibility is required in using position descriptions, as well as a good measure of Christian charity. Having your particular assignment spelled out for you in writing is supposed to help you and your church function more effectively. It should not be misconstrued as an instrument of oppression which will force people to produce. Position descriptions serve the larger purposes of the church and do nothing more. If the board becomes a slave to its documents, it can claim little more than the creation, from a state of chaos, where there is no definition, of a state of bondage, where there is too much documentation. Although concern over the vast amounts of paperwork is very appropriate in such large organizations as the federal government, most churches do not really have to be afraid of an impersonal bureaucracy as a result of written statements of accountability. As a matter of fact, we have found that the smaller the church, the more it needs to clarify in writing who is in fact responsible to whom for what. Unfortunately, most small churches have people with neither the time nor the talent necessary to make a commitment to such a system, and this includes the clergy. This is the case because the typical little congregation tends to operate in a style of "management by activity," which usually results in a program that attempts to respond to crisis after crisis as they occur. It would seem that only very large parishes, such as Trinity Church in New York City, ever really sustain themselves in a style of "management by objectives and results." Certainly one of your objectives should be the development of an effective local church administration, and to obtain this, keep in mind that documents are written on paper, not tablets of gold. Be willing to redefine responsibilities and to rewrite position descriptions as often as necessary. Sometimes this will involve you in developing entirely new functions which were once subfunctions in other areas. Whatever the situation, put it in writing, and then be prepared to rewrite it again and again in order that it might remain useful and helpful to your church's overall goals.

Our effort in preparing this book is really an example of us preaching what we practice. We have simply put into writing what we have discovered to be extremely valuable in our own experiences. Much of what we have to offer here is neither highly original nor terribly exciting. It really is rather basic, and because what we have done is so elementary and practical, we know you will find it to be a handy reference and guide. So make the most of our manual. Mark it up with notes which will make it applicable to your own situation. Write your own descriptions, using what you find in these pages as models. Read those parts which seem to have the most relevance for you, and skip those sections which do not seem to be of interest. It certainly is not our expectation that very many people will read this work from cover to cover, starting at the beginning and going straight through to the end, nor is it our purpose to be too academic or theological. Instead we have put together much "how-to-do-it" information which can be used to make your church organization more effective. What we have done has already worked very well for us, and we are sure it will do the same for you.

Although it is impossible to acknowledge our appreciation of everyone who has contributed to this effort in one way or the other, it also is impossible not to thank people from St. John's Church, Worcester, Massachusetts; St. Gregory's Church, Parsippany-Troy Hills, New Jersey; Calvary Church, Summit, New Jersey; St. Peter's Church, Livingston, New Jersey; and the Dioceses of Newark and Western Massachusetts.

As you make use of this manual, remember the biblical injunction that each separate part of the Body of Christ is to "work according to its function" (Ephesians 4:16). Until you have committed to paper the actual extent of each board member's function, you can hardly expect any significant degree of performance. Without written statements of accountability, your board is attempting to do the job without some of the necessary tools. Once you have developed your own set of written position descriptions, the members of your board will be freed from the handicap of not knowing the nature of their functions. Such freedom will allow for increased working capacities according to mutually agreed-upon standards.

HCL and JGP
New Jersey
August, 1976

CHAPTER ONE:

Church Organization In The Past

Any serious approach to the project of writing position descriptions should include a review of past practices of church organization in general and previous policies in particular. Such a historical review is important, if for no other reason than that it saves you from doing again what has already been done and has proven unproductive. Just how important it is to consider the past has been put plainly by George Santayana: "Those who cannot remember the past are condemned to repeat it."

So you will certainly want to recall past efforts in church organization. This chapter will help you in your historical review, but it will not provide a great deal of factual material. There are two reasons for our abridging the data. First, we have found not too much to be readily available. Church organization is not a subject about which a great amount has been written. Secondly, what has been done in this area seems to have little application to a church's struggle for survival in our contemporary culture of conflict and change. For example, Fenn's *Parish Administration*, last published in 1951, is extremely dated and only of value to a collector.

EARLY CHURCH ORGANIZATION

During the first few centuries of the Church a great deal of time was spent on theological matters. There was a need to formulate accurate statements about Christ's divine and human nature. You can read for yourself about the great Councils in Nicaea (325 A.D.), Constantinople (381 A.D.), Ephesus (431 A.D.), and Chalcedon (451 A.D.). None of these formal meetings of the whole Church did much in the way of church organization. There was of course a structure which developed around the apostles and later bishops who held authority as overseers and chief evangelists in a designated area. Locally, congregations came to be assigned presbyters who functioned much like the governing board of elders in Jewish communities of the day. A third order in the ministry was also local in nature. This group started with the appointment of seven men by the apostles, and they came to be known as deacons, who were charged with the responsibility of administering the charity work and care to the widows, orphans, and poor. The deacons were really the first administrators in the church organization, even though there were neither properties nor organized memberships as there are today. This threefold structure of bishops, priests, and deacons came to be the recognized order of ministries, which is still in use in the Orthodox, Catholic, and Anglican branches of the Church today. Nineteen centuries ago, however, there was only a common faith in the lordship of Christ that kept Christians together in units of various sizes. There was not really any thought of commitment to an organization.

After the persecutions by the Roman Empire ceased, Christianity grew at such a rapid rate that the primitive administrative system which relied heavily on the deacon was no longer sufficient. The bishop, whose office became firmly established around the middle of the second century, had to further delegate responsibilities, and so the full duties of a congregation were assumed by parish priests who were given local ecclesiastical jurisdiction to function on behalf of the bishop. This parochial structure formed the basis of a diocesan or geographical structure, which in turn became the constituent element in provincial, synodical, and larger systems. Each layer of the early Church's hierarchy generated more and more definite controls, all of which were modeled after the civil system of the Roman Empire. This pattern of the Church shaping itself structurally in imitation of secular institutions has been followed right down to our own time.

For instance the Episcopal Church follows similar lines of organization used unsuccessfully by our country under the Articles of Confederation from 1781 to 1788, and the National Council of Churches has test marketed a financial collection plan for local congregations in the 1970's similar to the Automatic Bank Check programs used by insurance companies to receive direct payment of premiums from their clients' bank accounts.

In 313 A.D. the Edict of Milan clearly established the Church and put it under government protection. Charles Merrill Smith rightly identifies the fourth century as the beginning of the church corporation, and it was not too long before Christian standards found their way into government legislation. The entire life of the Roman Empire was affected. Still, church involvement in secular affairs was for the most part carried on by the ordained ministers. The members of the church had very limited influence and were not to have an opportunity for administrative participation at a significant level for almost a thousand years.

Between the fall of the Roman Empire and the fifteenth century is the story of the Middle Ages in Europe, at the end of which the Church of England was formed. You can read for yourself a very excellent synopsis of these times in Powel Mills Dawley's *Chapters In Church History*. Before the Reformation in England was complete every aspect of political, economic, and social life had influenced Anglicanism, which is known in this country as the Episcopal Church.

Our abbreviated historical review is particularly selective at this point because of the many events which took place in the break away from the Papal State and the gradual evolution and development of Anglicanism. One fact that became paramount over the changing years was the eventual predominance of a secular pluralism. This variety of worldly values was certainly not apparent to those caught up in the Reformation and the Counter-Reformation, and it is really only now that the church is experiencing the full blast of a world whose values are largely determined by material advantages. In such a context more and more control is being exercised by the ninety-nine per cent of the Church who are *not* ordained ministers. This is particularly the case in mainline Protestant churches in this country, of which the Episcopal Church is a good example. Such lay participation at every level of church life is surely due in part to the concept of the separation of church and state. A vitality and a need for participation of all the members of a congregation has characterized church life in America since the landing at Plymouth Rock. You only have to consider the Church of England, the established state church, with its extremely large inactive membership to appreciate the importance of church development and lay involvement in a congregation which functions independently of the political structure.

ENGLISH DEVELOPMENT

In the Episcopal Church the governing body concerned with local church administration is referred to as a vestry for a parish and as an executive committee for a mission. The word "vestry" really designates a room where vestments are kept, and in the early days of lay participation in the sixteenth century the group of church officers actually met in the vesting room or vestry to conduct the necessary business of the parish church. Although this English term came into general use in the American Church, the functions and responsibilities of an Episcopalian vestry do not correspond exactly to those of an English one. This difference is due in part to the establishment status of the Church of England.

During the Middle Ages we first find records of church wardens, who were supposed to keep the nave in good repair. Interestingly, wardens were not allowed in the chancel and the sanctuary, since these areas were reserved for the ordained ministers. Since the early years of the fifteenth century wardens have been designated as the chief lay officers in English parishes. In addition, English bishops appointed certain laymen to report periodically on the state of their respective congregations. These appointees were known as questmen. Later they were known as synodsmen, since they reported at synod meetings, and subsequently the bishops' appointees became known simply as sidesmen.

Thus was the way opened for the laity to become involved in the affairs of the congregation. In time general recognition was given to the parishioners' responsibility to defray the cost of repairs to the church buildings and the upkeep of the church yard, furniture, fabric, books, and vestments. This acceptance of accountability on the part of the membership helped the parish officers to clarify their own functions and responsibilities, which resulted in the warden becoming a very familiar position in the local English church.

Just as wardens took on the responsibilities of parochial affairs, so too did vestries, even going so far as to levy church rates for upkeep and protection of properties. Not until the Local Church Act of 1894 was the civil authority of English rural vestries superseded by parochial church councils and annual parish meetings, and another five years went by before the London Government Act transferred authority from urban congregations to metropolitan boroughs with the mayor, aldermen, and council assuming responsibilities previously managed by vestries of city churches.

AMERICAN DEVELOPMENT

By the time the Episcopal Church was established in this country, there was already a long tradition of local church administration based on lay participation with a board or vestry and officers or wardens. The typically English concept of a Rector's Warden and the Peoples' Warden was gradually replaced in America by the notion of a senior and a junior warden, which to this day has no official sanction in the laws or canons of the Episcopal Church. As a matter of practice today, many congregations do not make much of a distinction as to which of their wardens is senior and junior. Usually the one in office the longer time is thought of as the senior officer.

Since the warden exercises a key role in the life of the congregation as a leader and steward, much care must be taken in his selection. His relationship to the vestry might be thought of as the "whip" or the one who guides his fellow vestrymen and women into a concern for the total well-being of the Church and not just simply for the nuts-and-bolts, day-to-day operation. A preoccupation with local affairs is a potential problem for every warden and vestry to face. Unless an interest and a participation in the life of the diocese, including a good working relationship with the bishop, is constantly emphasized, a cancerous parochialism will ultimately destroy the most effective church organization.

After the Revolutionary War there was real confusion over the position and responsibilities of the vestry in a disestablished or "free" Church. Their rights, duties, and relationships needed redefinition, but it took the young Church almost one hundred years even to appoint a commission to study and report on the several functions of Rector, Warden, and Vestrymen and their control and administration of parishes. The General Convention of 1877 began a serious attempt to define proper channels of accountability, which was finally formulated into Canon 13—"Of Parish Vestries" —in 1904. You can read this canon for yourself in the Appendix I at the back of this book (page 78). It is one rather dramatic example of how long it can take to clarify and change a confused state of affairs.

Now you should know the Church can and does change, even if somewhat slowly at times. Structures in the local church continue to adjust and apply new designs and systems developed in business and industry. For example, the pocket calculator and its big brother, the computer, have become invaluable analytical tools for churches to use in assessing financial performance. In the development of effective church management with the increased participation of the laity, the influence of modern management methods is being felt, as lay men and women seek to apply secular systems of efficiency. Such an application has certainly been stimulated by rising costs of goods and services and by a corresponding decrease in membership. With the ever-present possibility of taxation, effective property utilization is but one area in which increased responsibility is required of the laity. Yet in small congregations, additional volunteer hours are often unavailable. Also, in some churches the engagement of a full-time priest is not possible. In either case, this has meant fewer people having to do more, and that can only come about through increased effectiveness, which we have found to be directly related to clear written statements about who is to do what for whom by when.

We conclude our historical review by observing that church organization has indeed come a long way from the early years of the church when deacons were in charge of what administration there was for the widows, orphans, and poor. There has been a development which has become more and more obvious during the last four centuries, and that is the increasing need for lay participation and concern. History has shown a clergy-dominated church to be largely irrelevant and particularly ineffective in church organization. You have much to contribute, and your talents can be a great help in effective local church administration. We believe a team effort of clergy and laity is required these days, along with a clear understanding of the needs and assignments that must be fulfilled for the good of the Body of Christ.

CHAPTER TWO:

Church Organization In Principle

As you reflect on the nature of the functions and responsibilities you will want to include in your position description, we believe you will find it helpful to be aware of the fourfold functions that are distinguishable in any structured system: planning, organizing, motivating, and controlling. *Planning* entails establishing priorities and objectives based on a specific set of values, as well as developing effective delivery systems and routines or means which will accomplish the specified goals or ends. *Organizing* refers to the process whereby the available resources of people, capital, and equipment are mobilized and utilized for the sake of the organizational objectives. *Motivating* is a term used to explain the "why" of a person's actions and can be related to both the quantity and the quality of an individual's performance. The *controlling* function has to do with monitoring results or with the follow-up procedures which measure actual achievements against anticipated ones and which allow for alternative actions to compensate and correct deviations. These various functions are of course all highly interrelated and are usually experienced and exercised simultaneously, although at any given time we have found one function usually receives more emphasis and attention than the others. In *Management of Organizational Behavior,* Hersey and Blanchard use the following diagram (page 5) to illustrate the multiplicity in the unity of the fourfold function. Note how each function influences and is dependent upon the other three functions. For instance, planning must include provisions for obtaining the appropriate resources, encouraging participation and following up on the results. Without such provisions there is no planning function, and the same is true for organizing, motivating and controlling.

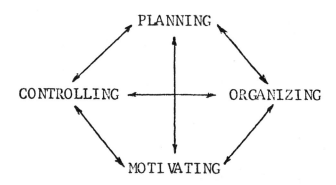

FIVE ORGANIZATIONAL STYLES

In addition to this fourfold functional understanding, you should also be aware of the type of structure or context which is predominant on your board and in your congregation. Peter Rudge, in *Ministry and Management*, first published in England in 1968, maintains all organizations operate in one of five styles: *traditional, charismatic, classical, human relations* and *systemic*. Each of these five operational styles refers to a specific and describable type of organizational structure and to a corresponding theory of management. For instance the *traditional structure* emphasizes a heritage which must be maintained at all costs. Such a commitment to keep the status quo intact casts you as a leader in the role of a preserver or curator. What this says to you in your own position is that your description will not only be limited but must be defined in terms of your church's chief operational style and goals. So the *charismatic type* of church conceives itself giving effect to the intuition of the Holy Spirit and allowing for spontaneous creativity and change, and your position description, to be most effective, would require a great deal of flexibility in order to handle an ever-fluid state of affairs. In the *classical type* of church organization goals and objectives are perceived as quantitative factors which can be attained by maximizing efficiency, and here, for example, you would have to take into account a high concern for numbers in terms of family units, attendance, and income, with the quality of interpersonal and spiritual relationships being a secondary factor at best. On the other hand, a *human relations type* of parish exhibits a primary interest in the individual and his satisfaction within a network of relationships, and in such a situation your position description would do best to emphasize a sensitivity to peoples' levels of needs. The *systemic* or *organic* church structure reflects a type of organization with a high degree of integration and interdependence, which is extremely responsive to a changing and complex external and internal environment. Such a comprehensive organizational style would require you to concentrate on detecting and interpreting change, as well as integrating your findings into the ongoing life and ministry of the church as a whole.

Obviously these five styles are ideal forms which serve as analytical models in helping you to understand your own church's structure as it really exists. No doubt you will find a mixture in your own situation, and the larger your parish the more subsystems you will encounter with differing styles of their own. Your women's group or altar guild might very well be run in a rather traditional/classical mode, while a young mothers' group or prayer fellowship might function more in a charismatic/human relations style, while again your vestry might be somewhat systemic in its overall approach. The point we want to stress here is that perhaps the single most important factor for you to consider in writing your position description is the context, the organizational style, in which you will be exercising your function.

You have been actively involved in your congregation long enough to appreciate just how really unique parish life is. Its organization of people and their network of relationships, of capital, and of equipment, drawn together in a free and voluntary system in order to achieve a specific set of objectives often referred to as "Christian Living," is identifiable as separate and distinct from other organizational church structures, such as: an assembly, council, diocese, district, region, synod; from other voluntary services groups, such as: the YM/YWCA's, Boys' and Girls' Clubs, hospital volunteers, scouts, civic clubs; and from other non-voluntary organizations, such as: the Armed Services, commercial and industrial companies, governmental agencies, schools, etc. The parish organization itself in turn is composed of a variety of subsystems from the governing board to a choir and perhaps to a bridge or sewing club. In each of these subsystems effective leadership will most likely be exercised using different styles.

YOUR MINISTER IN THE CHURCH SYSTEM

In all the mixture of styles in your church the position of chief minister, pastor, or rector is obviously critical in terms of the total life of the parochial system. Surely you realize the way in which your pastor exercises his function by the example and style he exhibits will to a large degree frame the values, sanctions, norms, and goals of your congregation as a whole. This is the case by virtue of the ordained minister's position in the formal organization of your parish, where his ideas are always expected, even if they are not always accepted. His influence in the decision making process of the parochial system and its subsystems is vast by the weight of church polity and his own training. He is expected to get things done, even if he is not always as successful or as effective as he and the members of his parish might wish. This power, which in most parochial settings comes with the job, is not directly derived from any divine source. In a very real sense God does not make a "boss," but churches do! Your pastor derives his functional authority from the total ecclesiastical organization in which he is expected to function. This authority is certainly contingent upon the support of the local membership, but in many denominations, including the Episcopal Church, the source of organizational power is actually centered in a traditional/classical hierarchy with certain duties being assigned to the parish minister. For instance Canon 20—"Of Ministers and Their Duties"— clearly states that the minister in charge has "control" of worship and parish buildings, as well as spiritual jurisdiction. You will of course find some local variations and exceptions in which a pastor may in fact function at the pleasure of the congregation as a whole, but such instances are confined to a few Protestant denominations and are often the result of the congregation's original charter and bylaws. The point here is that your pastor, like most chief ministers, is required to function as the chief executive officer.

Depending on which study is chosen, such as Samuel Blizzard's in 1956 or Alfred Shands's in 1970, you should be aware that your pastor spends at least 50% of his time each week engaged in various functions of management! Do you find this to be surprising? It is not so startling when you realize that your hierarchy in effect requires your pastor to function as an executive operations manager with appropriate management responsibilities. There are the many meetings of all sorts and conditions, the behind the scenes meetings and preparations for meetings, and the hours spent in personal communication and on the telephone. Your pastor will employ the fourfold functions in such parish activities as the stewardship or canvass program, your annual dinner and social, the special Lenten services, the building and/or organ fund drive. Now to enable the parish minister to have more available time to function in the areas of pastoral counseling, parish calling, and other "religious" programs, some congregations engage a full- or part-time office manager or lay administrator to take some of the daily management load off the minister, but such a professional worker does not mean that the clergyman can abdicate his overall responsibility. Effective oversight of staff must be maintained in order to ensure accomplishment of organizational objectives. Indeed, no matter how much time your pastor spends in administration, whether or not he has professional or volunteer administrative assistance, most denominations with hierarchical organization require through their tradition and rules that the local minister in charge is "the man," the one to whom people of the congregation and members of the community look for support and guidance in order to carry out their own functions within the organizational structure of the church.

Within this framework your pastor provides opportunities for people in your congregation and community to minister to one another, which can be the minister's most significant contribution. The parish minister must be concerned with authenticating and affirming the individual's inherent integrity as a steward in his own right within the community of the people of God. This concern is not to be confused with delegating or authorizing a person to act for others. Your pastor should not so much be sending people to act on his behalf, as he should be making it possible for people to act on their own. In other words, the pastor should use his position in the hierarchical structure to serve as a catalyst, in the original sense of the word, to dissolve, disband, and destroy barriers, so that the people of God, such as yourself, may function on the basis of the inspiration of the Holy Spirit.

To be a catalyst requires working with and through individuals and groups to accomplish organizational goals. This is what we understand Christian management to be: functioning in the context of interpersonal relationships for the sake of the Gospel of Jesus Christ. Both your pastor and you, as well as the other members on your board, must be good managers and stewards of the mysteries of God. Being effective in local church administration means achieving an integration of the various fourfold functions: planning, organizing, motivating and controlling. Bishop Stewart tells us in his unpublished M.B.A. thesis (page 5):

Administration is required to accelerate the flow from the upper part of the hour glass . . . to the lower part.

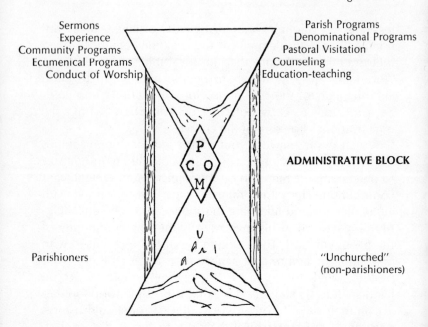

Sermons
Experience
Community Programs
Ecumenical Programs
Conduct of Worship

Parish Programs
Denominational Programs
Pastoral Visitation
Counseling
Education-teaching

ADMINISTRATIVE BLOCK

Parishioners

"Unchurched"
(non-parishioners)

The ADMINISTRATIVE BLOCK refers to the role which you and your pastor must perform in order to carry out your other various functions in church and community. The letters "P, O, M, C" in the diamond represent the fourfold functions operative in any organization. This model of an hour glass also illustrates the reciprocity and the state of a dynamic give and take between the upper and lower parts of the figure. The point of this diagram is to indicate the very critical function which management fulfills in serving as a sort of power tool enabling a church to accomplish what would otherwise require an even larger expenditure of time and effort. If you are interested in some of the specific techniques involved in good church management, we know no book to be more comprehensive than Bishop William A. Lawrence's classic, *Parsons, Vestries, & Parishes: A Manual.*

PLANNING, ORGANIZING, MOTIVATING AND CONTROLLING

If you look closely at the administrative block, which is apparent in so many congregations, particularly small ones, the skill with which the fourfold function is exercised is directly related to the flow between programs and people. Therefore, we conclude this chapter with a brief discussion of each of these functions.

Planning has to do with putting first things first, and that means establishing goals, objectives, priorities, and procedures. Yet before you can get going on goal identification, let alone achievement, attention must be given to the quality and maintenance of interpersonal relationships within the congregation. Never assume that a level of trust and a climate of co-operation and understanding exists and never fall into the trap of thinking that such matters will take care of themselves. We have found that to maintain an effective team requires a definite position, which we have termed the persononel function. Without building into your parish's structure a group whose job it is to ensure continually good working relationships, you will gain only a short-lived church organization, which will become increasingly ineffective as people come and go.

All this is especially true given the nature of the parish structure as a voluntary association. The degree of effectiveness of any parish is a direct result of the ability of its members to work well together for common goals and in support and satisfaction of individual needs. Both the attainment of organizational goals and the satisfaction of individual needs are necessary for the life of the parish as a whole. Indeed, this is true for any group or organization. Without organizational objectives there is no context within which individuals can be related. There has to be a reason for people to come together and to stay together; however, provided such a rationale does exist, no matter how vague, there must also be a concern to maintain the group of people so gathered.

This maintenance function is distinct from any other task function, and neither this nor other objectives can be pursued exclusively, given an overall concern for the well-being of a congregation. In this concern individual needs must be given serious consideration. If a person's needs as a member are not being fulfilled, his performance or lack of it will ultimately reflect his own feelings of frustration, anger, and hostility. These feelings will certainly have their influence. As a steward you must be sure a dynamic is developed in your congregation which takes into account task, maintenance of the group, and individual needs. So since one of the objectives of any church is the development of interpersonal relationships in the Name of Jesus Christ, the first planning objective will always be people. After all, people represent a means and an end in their own persons and in the Church.

To be effective, do your planning with people and not for them. Involve as many people from your congregation as you possibly can in the planning process, as well as in reviews and evaluations. We have found a parish-wide goal identification and achievement program to be most helpful. By giving everyone the opportunity through personal write-in participation to respond to the question, "What would make parish life more meaningful for you?", you can accurately determine what programs will be most beneficial. Quite a number of parishes and missions in the Diocese of Newark have found such an exercise to be most helpful, and if you pay similar attention to people's needs your planning should become a continual and co-operative venture.

Organizing refers to matching up available resources with specified objectives, and although your parish no doubt has a variety of assets at its disposal, from its physical facilities to its funds or capital, the lives, interests, and capabilities of the people who are in fact the parish itself constitute the most valuable asset. Indeed, the most accurate way to understand the nature of the parochial structure is to view it as the people of God and the ministers of Christ in a particular location, where your pastor is simply one among many who exercises the fourfold functions. Without people there can be no church anywhere. In assessing your parish's resources then, the basic question is not "What do we need to do so and so?", but "Who can do so and so?" Too much emphasis cannot be placed on people as opposed to things. A congregation rich with people seems to be able to uncover other resources as required, whereas an impoverished parish is one not so much lacking in material resources as it is in people committed to the faith and inspired by the Holy Spirit. So if you are in a small church with less than one hundred active families, your major organizing effort will have to be in terms of recruitment and membership. Otherwise you may seriously have to consider joining hands with another little congregation nearby in order to be a truly effective and viable parochial unit.

Your organizing function will also require you to be aware of the degree of utilization of your parish's assets. For instance, it is one matter to involve your entire board in a telephone canvass for a church supper which turns out 10% of the congregation; however, a more effective approach and a higher utilization level might be achieved by involving one well-liked member who has the time to make all the calls and who could possibly turn out 20% of the people. Your total of volunteer hours must always be weighed against anticipated results. In addition, your organizing function will require you to consider distribution. It is no use having all your assets perfectly utilized if they are being employed at the wrong end of town from where the need exists. It is one matter to use well and wisely who and what is available; it is quite another story to be where you are needed when you are needed.

In working with the assets which belong to the people who make up the membership of your parish, one of the most useful approaches you can implement is that of team building. It has been clearly shown, for instance, that group decision making performance is more accurate and productive than individual results. Also, the effectiveness of a group in attaining its objectives is considerably higher than that of any of its individual members. This is so because the total system is more than a mere sum of its parts, and in fact has a life of its own. If your parish does not yet function as a team, in a spirit of collaboration instead of competition, then you are equally responsible with your pastor and colleagues to organize this very important area of church life.

One other extremely valuable asset in your church is time. In order to accomplish anything at all, it is necessary to take into consideration the available volunteer hours which can be effectively utilized. Obviously your fellow parishioners are not being paid for their time, which is really an inestimable gift. Make sure people's time is well used. Peter Drucker, the high priest of modern management, puts the matter this way in *The Effective Executive* (page 33):

> People-decisions are time-consuming, for the simple reason that the Lord did not create people as "resources" for organization. They do not come in the proper size and shape for the tasks that have to be done in organization—and they cannot be machined down or recast for these tasks. People are always "almost fits" at best. To get the work done with people (and no other resource is available) therefore requires lots of time, thought, and judgment.

Quite obviously the point here is that "no other resource is available." The effective use of human resources in the parochial system will be your central problem and challenge.

Motivating refers to internal inertia, or to one's drive and desire for achievement. As a leader in your parish, you cannot afford to overlook the necessity to provide an environment which will stimulate people into action. Such a climate requires an effective communications system. In the Church such a system or network has to do more than merely provide data to a group of people. It has to make it possible for a sharing of feelings as well as ideas. It has to function in such a way that there can be free, open, and honest exchanges between individuals, individuals and groups, and groups. This network will not work without considerable and continual effort. It is itself a major parish program, and the success of developing really good communication all the way around will to a large extent indicate the degree of success that can be expected from other parish projects. Communication certainly does not always mean agreement, but it does mean a willingness to listen and to respond openly and honestly. It also means increased opportunities for people in the parish to respond to parochial objectives and programming.

Communication is not the only example of a support system in the church which stimulates motivation. Another area is transportation or delivery systems. Any parish project is not developed simply for its own sake but for the benefit of people, and so a corollary to planning any project is to plan the means whereby it can be supplied or delivered to people. In industry such distinct functions as marketing and public relations have evolved to enhance the capacity of a company to deliver its products readily to the consumer, and although most local congregations do not have such sophistication, nevertheless, there must be a concern with the means by which it gets the message across, as well as with the content. A very obvious example of a congregational transportation system has to do with providing the means whereby anybody who wants to come to worship services on a Sunday will be able to get to church. In East Boston in the 1960's several local churches recognized the need to provide some kind of transportation for the many people who did not have cars and who were either too old or too young to walk the distances across busy streets. There was no real bus service, and so the congregations got together and pooled their limited assets to hire a private bus which made the rounds of the area picking up and dropping off passengers at the different churches. The concern expressed by the churches to take an interest in people getting to worship easily and safely was reflected in an increase in participation and attendance. In a way this bus project can be viewed as a motivational incentive. People were stimulated to think that such trouble on the part of the churches deserved use, and they thought they were helping to make good use of an opportunity which had been provided initially to meet their needs. Needless to say, transportation systems are themeslves messages of care and concern, as well as messengers, to which people can readily respond.

In your attempts to motivate, to mobilize action, remember that people motivate themselves. You are merely providing a stimulating environment in which people's capacity to respond can be maximized. Mobilization involves putting together people and ideas, materials and money, institutions and agencies with influence and feelings to produce results in the form of concrete programs and changes in people's lives and behavior. To a large degree your strategy of mobilization and motivation will be one which encourages the establishment of an environment which will provide the potential for need satisfaction and a sense of well-being. It will enable your fellow parishioners to actualize their respective individual ministries fully. Ultimate need satisfaction is in terms of self-actualization, and in the Church this is understood in terms of relationships with God, other people, and one's own self, and in terms of the ministry of all those who are baptized in the Name of Christ Jesus. Your parish environment is or should be so designed and structured toward this end.

Controlling involves working with the results. For results there must be follow-through. In such sports as golf and tennis the final part of the stroke after the ball has been hit makes all the difference in whether or not the hit is effective and produces the desired result. That is to say, as much energy has to be expended on the follow-through as on the actual contact. Similarly, you and your pastor must work every bit as hard after a new program has been implemented as you did in planning, organizing, and motivating it into operation. You must see to it that whatever project is started continues to accomplish the objectives for which it was originally intended, and when the project begins *not* to correspond with expectations, you must do one of two things: either make adjustments in performance so that the original objectives are maintained or else revise the objectives in the light of actual performance. Both courses of action require a continuing interest and concern. You can never really walk away and leave the pot cooking, expecting it to take care of itself. This means that in exercising the planning function the control function must be taken into account. In the very process of planning, anticipated deviations must be noted. If you do not do your potential problem analysis before it is needed, you will wind up doing it after you have a real emergency on your hands.

None of this is meant to imply that a heavy-handed or manipulative approach is desirable in exercising the control function. Indeed a constant checking up on matters can be counterproductive in eliciting such feelings as "he-doesn't-trust-me-so-why-should-I-bother?" The other extreme can also bring similar results and feelings of "he-doesn't-care-enough-to-see-how-I'm-doing-so-why-should-I-bother?" Somewhere between these two extremes a style of control must be developed in your congregation which is both humanizing and faithful to the larger organizational goals of your parish. In the Church such a style emphasizes internal personal responsibility within the corporate community in which everyone shares in the control function of making sure there is congruence between plan and progress.

Dealing with follow-through will invariably involve you in conflicts and crises. The givenness of all kinds of differences cannot be ignored, and you and your board must develop systems which will make positive use out of so-called negative situations. A disruption must be seen as more than an annoyance and accepted as a potentially valuable means for improvement. Actually it is people's response of either aggression or repression, of either resisting or avoiding, which can be so destructive. It is people's secondary feelings

about their hurt or anger that may make a situation intoler-
able. Conflicts and crises are in themselves no more negative than any other aspect of life, and in fact provide a very
effective feedback system. If people have little to say about
how things are going in your congregation, you really have
less to respond to than if there were loud cries of dissatisfac-
tion. For example, if your educational committee introduced
a new program which received a hostile and angry response
from people who were quite pleased with what you had
been doing, this feedback would provide additional data
which would perhaps require a restructuring of the program
or a re-evaluation of objectives. If on the other hand people
were to repress their feelings, believing it not nice to dis-
agree, the resultant tension, unacknowledged, could very
well bring about a collapse of the entire parish, as well as
the new educational program. What we are saying here is
that from the perspective of systems control, opposition
offers the possibility of correction before there is a complete
breakdown. It is only when opposition is not taken as a
warning signal that results are really adversely affected. Hostility especially is a symptom that something is out of hand,
that someone is hurt, and that immediate attention is required. Crises are not so much in response to a given situation as they are the result of given situations in which secondary feelings have caused a block in communication. Your
parish, perhaps through a personnel committee, must develop a degree of flexibility that will enable it to handle
such stress experiences when they occur.

Very rarely will you enjoy the luxury of being able to concentrate exclusively on one of the fourfold functions in the
church. You will continually be planning and organizing,
motivating and controlling, all at the same time. You will
continually be called upon to work on different projects
simultaneously, during which you will no doubt be exercising different functions on different projects at any given
time. Does this sound like too much? It could be, and it is
precisely because of the many demands on your time that

we have written this book as your handy guide. We have found written position descriptions to be an excellent strategy in producing a church organization that is highly flexible and capable. If you take our lead and write down *who is responsible for what to whom by when,* then you will have given yourself more time to operate an effective local church administration by developing a fourfold functional approach.

CHAPTER THREE:

Church Organization By The Book

One of the basic principles in organization, which is usually neglected in churches, is that structure is a function of purpose. We cannot emphasize to you too much the importance of this concept. Whatever policies your board makes, whatever decisions are made, and whatever programs are developed will to some degree reflect either explicit or implicit goals. Your congregation's structure, the way it goes about its business, is a nonverbal message that tells members and anyone else who thinks about it what are in fact the values, norms, and sanctions by which your parish functions. For instance a church which acts on the basis of consensus decisions functions in a way which is perfectly compatible with the biblical concept of a priesthood of all believers. On the other hand a board which acts without ever consulting the congregational membership at large would be frustrating any significant development of participation. Quite simply, we have found that what and how churches *do* their job speaks louder and clearer than what is actually said. Often this means conflicting and confusing messages! Not only do many churches fail to develop and maintain precise purpose statements by which they can measure the effectiveness of their structure, there is also a general lack of interest in congruence between the medium and the message.

One area we have found to be particularly overlooked by local churches is the formal canonical and civil law structure. It would seem little attention is paid to ensuring real compatibility between the legal statements to which the church organization is supposed to conform and the overall purposes either written or otherwise for which it exists and functions. For example there is a strong emphasis these days on total participation by the laity, the 99% of the Church. One canon in the Episcopal Church both affirms and denies such a concept in the same sentence! It appears that a congregation formally designated as a "parish," an autonomous congregation financially independent in union with a diocesan convention, is legally required by church law to prepare and deliver an annual report which is "the joint duty of the Rector and Vestry." Yet in every other congregation, such as a mission which is dependent financially and otherwise on a diocese, this same report is the sole "duty of the Minister in charge thereof." Structure is a function of purpose indeed, and here *it* would seem there is an implicit design which makes a rather sharp distinction between a parish and a mission and which designates more responsibility to people in parishes than in missions. In fact this is not necessarily the case at all, and in many missions there is a very real collaborative effort on the part of the priest and the Executive Committee, including joint preparation and delivery of an annual report. Still such action is not by the book. The canonical structure here clearly needs some redefinition. You can form your own opinion on this by reading for yourself the Canon entitled "Of The Mode Of Securing An Accurate View Of The State Of This Church" in Appendix I (page 75).

Although love for God, neighbor, and self is a prime concern for the church, most of the ecclesiastical and civil law connected with congregations has to do with matters of finance and assets, like any other corporation. The Canon "Of Business Methods In Church Affairs," also reproduced in Appendix I (page 75), is very specific. Yet time and time again Episcopal churches large and small ignore such a straightforward procedure as an annual certificate of audit, which is to be forwarded to the Bishop or Ecclesiastical Authority not later than July 1 of each year. We would certainly think it a loving thing to do to make sure our hard working treasurers were well protected from any hint of impropriety.

We see such a canonical requirement of an annual audit to be a structure which is highly congruent to the overall purposes of the church.

As you review your church's book of rules and regulations, constitution and charter, bylaws and canons, note the implicit purposes and policies embodied in those statements of procedures which provide the structure for your congregation. For instance in the Episcopal Church the canon makes it very clear that no property of any Parish, Mission, Congregation, or Institution in a diocese can be encumbered or alienated "without the written consent of the Bishop and Standing Committee." Such a canon suggests that in effect there is really no such thing as an "independent" parish in the Episcopal Church, at least with respect to property. The implication of this legal structure supports the Catholic concept of the diocese as the basic unit of the church.

While it must be recognized that the diversity of the modern church, the transportation revolution in this century, and the concentration of different and unique congregations in the same geographical area, especially urban centers, all suggest the need for a more flexible canon on who is a member of what parish, still, one of the more loving traditional canons in the Episcopal Church is the one which has to do with jurisdiction and the defining of parochial boundaries. It was Aristotle who made the point that the child to whom everyone is a parent really has no one. So it is in congregations. Unless there is an agreement as to which parish serves which area and which clergyman is responsible for the spiritual charge and pastoral care of which people, overall effectiveness will be marginal, and the needs of many may go unfulfilled. Hence we see a canon which is concerned about who is responsible for whom in a given geographical area as a legal statement about church organization which is highly compatible with the Church's basic purpose.

Not every canon can be plumbed for some deeper sense

of meaning. Some ecclesiastical and civil laws are on the books simply to document various parts of the church's organizational structure. For example the Canon "Of Parish Vestries" really does little more than to point out that "the Vestry shall be agents and legal representatives of the Parish in all matters concerning its corporate property and the relations of the Parish to its Clergy." The concept here is of course that some of the people represent all of the people most of the time in property and personnel matters. There is nothing in this idea which is either strongly supportive or terribly destructive of the essential nature of the Church.

We have found many Church members to be somewhat surprised that there are "regulations respecting the laity." The fact that the Episcopal Church's canon on this is so little known and so widely ignored suggests to us that perhaps here is a place where some attention is required to bring actual practice and church organization by the book into line. Moreover, distinctions between baptized members and communicants would appear to be more confusing than ever with the redevelopment in many areas of administering first communion to young children. Yet instead of adopting regulations which might be more helpful, very often dated canons are simply kept on the books. When this happens, Church structure continues to be unduly influenced by anachronistic ecclesiastical and civil laws. All this is to advise you to be as familiar as you can with the rules. You cannot change them until you know them, and you should never get stuck playing a game without knowing the rules. It is frustrating, to say the least!

YOUR CHURCH'S LEGAL IDENTITY

Before leaving this subject we think it important for you to be aware that your state also has a body of statutes which govern and provide for religious associations. While each state is somewhat different there is a common civil concern for the proper organization and function of a congregation as a corporation. In Appendix II (page 81) you can read portions of the New Jersey Statutes, which serve as an example to indicate the type of factors spelled out in civil law. Did you know that in New Jersey it is legal for wardens to call a meeting of the vestry without the rector under certain conditions? Are you aware that in New Jersey it is necessary to have either a warden or two-thirds of the vestry present to constitute a quorum? Have you looked into what statutes in your state apply to your congregation? Some parishes are fortunate to have legal counsel available to them, and it would certainly be natural if you have a lawyer on your board to take advantage of his experience and skill. Nevertheless, legal structures, both ecclesiastical and civil, cannot be taken for granted in any effective local church administration, nor can responsibility for observing them be delegated and forgotten.

Whether or not your congregational membership includes a lawyer who would be willing to offer his services as a part of his Christian stewardship, it is important to have legal counsel readily available, perhaps through an able community attorney. We have found many circumstances in churches concerning legal requirements, conformity to local statutes, contracts, financial obligations and investments that demand expertise beyond the scope of the layman. You will find a friend in court to be an invaluable asset in the day-to-day business affairs of your church.

All major denominations are so structured that individual churches are legally incorporated entities either singly or collectively. Few people in your church are really aware of this legal fact of life, and even your colleagues on the board often only learn about your church's incorporation long after they have attended their first meeting. By being incorporated under state law, a congregation gains the legal status and rights of an individual. This means a church can make contracts, own property, and provide for its continued existence beyond the lifetime of those who formed the incorporated body. Such a continuity between the founding or charter members and succeeding generations is necessary when dealing with mortgages, bonds, building programs, and management of investments. Moreover the membership and officers in an incorporated congregation cannot be held personally liable for any bills or damages that might be caused in any way by the parish. From the perspective of corporate law, then, it is a good idea for your church membership to be aware they do not belong to either a club or a society, which in most states do not have any legal status and so cannot own property or make contracts unless they function under a trusteeship that can in some states be considered liable for debts and unpaid bills. This distinction between church membership and affiliation with a club or society is an important one, and we believe it to be a good example of corporate law as one type of church structure being a direct function of the purpose of the Church as the Body of Christ.

One final formal quasi-legal structure worth our mentioning is the set of bylaws that serve as a guide in your church's operation. Again not only will you find your fellow parishioners unaware of the contents of your bylaws, but you will also learn they are often totally ignorant of their very existence! Even though bylaws are unnecessary as a part of incorporation or for a Charter granted by a state, once established it is the responsibility of the congregation at its annual or special meeting to observe, maintain, and change them when required. Briefly the bylaws provide for the name and location of the congregation, scheduled time and place of meetings, composition of the membership and voter eligibility, quorum requirements in order to transact official business, titles of officers with their terms of office and election procedures, titles of committees and their functions, as well as provisions for amendments. We are sure you will find it helpful for everyone on your board to have an up-to-date copy of your bylaws in their manual, which also includes every member's position description along with other legal documents, such as a reproduction of your charter and statement of incorporation. Your mutually agreed upon statement as to the practices your board will follow can only serve as an effective guide if it is always easily available and constantly used and reviewed. Please do not take the time to write a guide book of bylaws if you do not intend to apply these actively as a real aid to effective local church administration. If your purpose is to develop and to maintain a well-run church organization, then we know you will want to build a structure in part by the book of your board's own composition, which will most certainly include a set of bylaws.

CHAPTER FOUR:

Church Organization In Detail

One very important visual aid or management tool for you to use in preparing your position description is the organization chart. Most congregations fail to make use of the classic chart with its boxes, lines, and dotted lines for the basic reason that such detail is too complex and too changeable. This is a case of doing the right thing for the wrong reason. The fact is that the classic organization chart is really not all that useful to the local congregation because its very structure of vertical-horizontal direct and indirect authority does very little to reflect the essential nature and purpose of the Church. Still, there is more than one way to illustrate graphically how people interact within a system. We have found that a circular organization chart very nicely indicates the overall interrelatedness among all the various functional parts of the local church. Such a detailed graphic representation serves you like a map, helping you to get your bearings and to find your way. Most of all such a circular chart is not all that difficult to create and maintain.

All of the position descriptions you will find in Appendix III (pages 83–111) can be quickly understood and easily remembered by developing a circular organizational concept using a single sheet of paper. Draw a large ring, and think of it as representing the total membership of your congregation and their authority as exercised at the annual meeting. Next add on an outside ring and divide it into two sections, indicating all the organizations in your church and the larger civil and ecclesiastical communities. Obviously the communities as well as the membership provide the people for your organizations, and this interrelatedness is illustrated by the two rings being next to each other. So far our circular organizational concept looks like this:

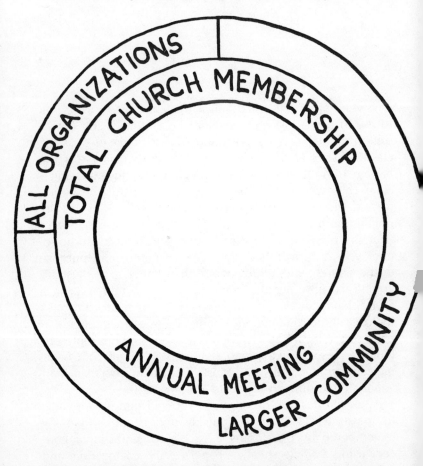

For our purposes here we are assuming your congregation is autonomous; however, if your church is a mission or dependent financially or otherwise on either another church or an ecclesiastical judicatory you might want to include this fact in your organizational concept by opening up your membership ring and adding a wedge as follows:

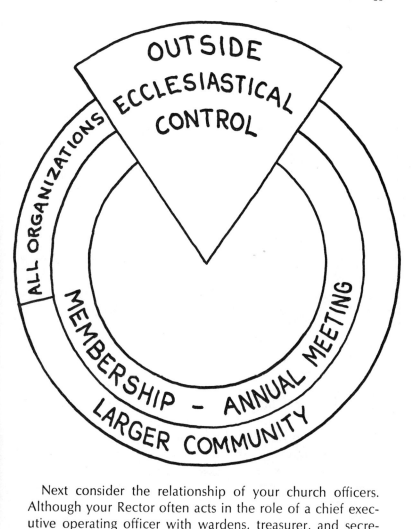

Next consider the relationship of your church officers. Although your Rector often acts in the role of a chief executive operating officer with wardens, treasurer, and secretary or clerk in a sense reporting to him, there is really a much more collegial arrangement in terms of the day to day affairs of your church. Instead of conceptualizing the "chain of command" as a vertical one with the Rector on top and the Wardens and Treasurer underneath, you will find it helpful to visualize a team at the core of the Vestry:

Just as it is critical for every member of your Vestry to be assigned a specific function with definite responsibilities, so it is equally vital for your officers to perform their respective duties on the basis of a written statement of expectations. Traditionally wardens were held accountable for finance and property only, while the Rector was expected to carry out programming and everything else. Such an arrangement is at best simply a rather poor use of available talent and at worst denies the laity any significant involvement in mission and ministry. If in fact every member of your congregation is a minister, then surely this means your chief lay officers ought to do more than simply keep things going for the Rector. We believe very strongly in a thorough doctrine of a priesthood of all believers, and that all Christians are called to specific ministries.

ADMINISTRATIVE AND PROGRAM RESPONSIBILITIES

You will find that it is important to assign wardens broad and major areas of responsibility. By such a division of labor clergy are enabled to concentrate and develop their own particular talents as ordained ministers while at the same time the laity is fully engaged in partnership with one another and with the clerical leadership.

Our experience has taught us that any matter or item of business which comes before your Vestry or Executive Committee can be readily categorized into one of two basic areas. Your board must deal with either administrative affairs or program considerations. There is really nothing else, and any subject is easily classifiable as either "administration" or "program." Such a duality in the church is really nothing unique. The Diocese of Newark has for a number of years distinguished between an annual diocesan program budget and an administrative budget; however, this concept has not only been undeveloped on the local church level, but it has also been widely by-passed in determining functional accountability at any level. This is due in part to the lack of detail and definition as to what constitutes an administrative or program item. Such a lack of clarity can be successfully attacked with a set of position descriptions which describe in detail who is to be responsible for what to whom by when. It really is a matter of documenting mutual understandings. We have found this can all be done quite handily by designating one of your wardens to be the chairman of an administrative department and the other to be chairman of the program department. This two-departmental approach to the work of your Vestry can be illustrated by making use of our circular organization concept:

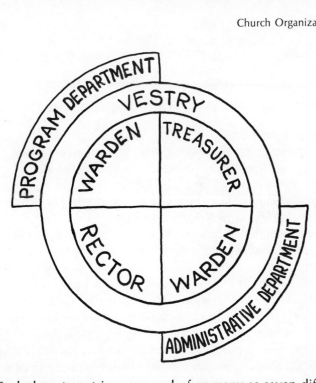

Each department is composed of as many as seven different functional areas, for each of which a specific member
of your Vestry or Executive Committee is accountable. In
smaller churches it might be necessary for one person to
exercise more than one function, but regardless of the size
of your church no one on your church board should be free
of some specific responsibility. The most disastrous results
occur on a team or with any group of people working together when a member has a free ride and a minimal commitment. You can avoid ineffectiveness by securing truly
committed people and making sure they are given real responsibility. In so doing you will be cultivating significant
lay ministries. Of course there is a potential liability with
this structure, and that is a certain degree of vulnerability.
If one of your board members is unable for whatever reason
to follow through on his function, it will be necessary for
the appropriate warden and committee to pick up the slack.

By developing different layers of function, responsibility,
and accountability there is a built-in system of checks and
balances, which will be required from time to time. Nevertheless, our experience with the two-department structure
has confirmed our belief in the efficacy of spreading or de-
centralizing authority as opposed to focusing or centralizing
it in the office of the Rector or in the hands of a "lay pope."
All this can be graphically represented so that the whole of
the local church can be understood in terms of its various
functional parts:

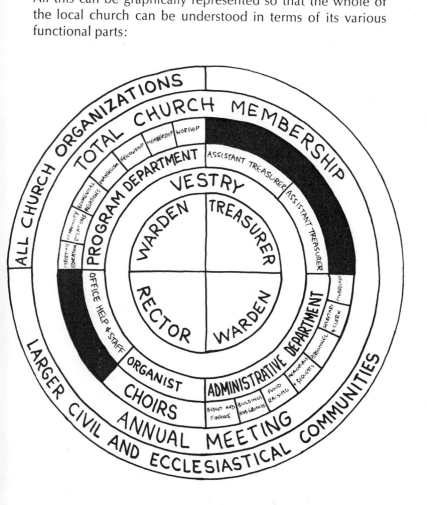

This organizational chart indicates that the officers are at the very center of functional accountability for the church, but that responsibility is actually exercised at all levels.

If for no other reason than the fact that your officers function as the hub of your local church wheel, there must be clear and written statements as to the mutual expectations of your Vestry or Executive Committee and its formal leadership. This is so for many other good reasons as well, from the perspective of good stewardship to the practice of good business. The purpose of role clarification through documentation is to help, not to hinder. Unfortunately this is not always the case, and when paper works gets in the way it is usually due to a lack of review and evaluation. Nevertheless, clergy are increasingly insisting on written agreements as a means by which to evaluate their own growth and performance.

In any contract you may develop with your Rector two items are essential beyond the usual considerations of salary, housing, and the like. *First*, a list of no more than five or six pastoral specialties should be prepared by as many people as possible from your congregation. Even though your Rector will be required from time to time to function in many different ways, a definite list will serve to give his ministry with you a distinct focus and emphasis. No one can do everything, and unless you specify some things that you want your spiritual leader to do well, he may end up doing nothing to anyone's satisfaction. In deriving your pastoral specialties list and having your personnel committee negotiate with your clergyman about it, you will surely find it most helpful to use a comprehensive listing similar to the one produced by the Clergy Deployment Office of the Episcopal Church and reprinted in Appendix III (page 83). *Secondly*, it is essential to make provisions for unanticipated adjustments and corrections in your clergyman's position description. It is simply impossible to be all-knowing and all-inclusive in any agreement, and so we have found it most beneficial to establish basic rules for the management of conflict *before* they are needed. Sooner or later you will differ with your spiritual leader. The only question is whether or not you and the Vestry will have previously agreed upon guidelines to use for a creative and effective resolution of the difference.

CHURCH BOARD CONCEPTS

You can see for yourself from our sample position descriptions that your two wardens are functionally accountable for the administration and program of your church. Obviously you need your most dedicated and committed leaders for these two pivotal positions. This dedication and commitment should be readily apparent to one and all in terms of weekly attendance, presence and participation in church activities and programs, and financial support which is regular and proportional to income. Wardens are in too central a position to be only nominal Christians and token givers. Indeed any member of your church board who doesn't believe in pledging and puts a dollar in the plate when he does come to church, not only sets a poor example for the congregation but seriously damages the overall effectiveness of your Vestry or Executive Committee. Misplaced responsibility can be devastating; so never make the mistake of placing big responsibilities in small hands! Go after people to be your officers who have really demonstrated their ability to handle church demands. Use your committees as proving grounds for developing leaders.

Although your Treasurer's primary function is obviously in terms of finance, this does not mean he or she can be excused from further participation on the Vestry team or in the life on the congregation. All too often church treasurers insulate and isolate themselves in order to do better work; however, part of any treasurer's job in a church is to work with people, encouraging and supporting them in any way possible. After all, the very funds for which your Treasurer is accountable come voluntarily from his peers. So do make sure your church Treasurer is one who will co-operate and work with fellow officers and board members. Your financial condition is just too important to be governed by a lone wolf or a maverick. A good Budget and Finance Committee can help a team player learn the details of the treasurer's office, but even the best of personnel committees would be extremely hard pressed to change a hard-nosed individualist who happens to be good at figures into a supportive board member.

Definition and detail for each department is contained within the various position descriptions, and although your board must produce its own statements, we have included samples in Appendix III (pages 83–111) to serve as models and guides. We have found that each of the fourteen areas that comprise the entire work of any Vestry or Executive Committee emphasizes a distinct and separate function requiring someone's personal attention. Do not neglect any of these fourteen functions simply beause they might seem unfamiliar. We conclude this chapter, therefore, with a brief commentary on and rationale for Vestry position descriptions.

Although the budget and finance function can include a fund raising function as well, we have found that it is much more desirable to keep the two separate. The former really serves as a corporate controllership, while the latter has a more narrow concern of increased income. Making sure that everyone in the congregation is kept advised of fiscal matters is more than enough of a job for a part-time volunteer. Similarly, when additional funds are required to balance you church's annual budget or to provide capital backing for a special project, you will need all the energies of a member of your Vestry working with a large number of church people. Still, if your circumstances are such that it is just impossible to operate these two functions separately, do make sure that the chairman of budget, finance, and fund raising has a reliable co-chairman who can manage one function when the other also needs attention.

Traditionally buildings and grounds work has been almost

the only work a Vestry did. Even today too many church boards spend entirely too much time dealing with matters that are best left in the hands of a capable committee chaired by a senior member of the congregation with experience in upkeep and maintenance. As long as your people are satisfied with the appearance and condition of your church facilities the only significant amount of time needed at your Vestry meetings for buildings and grounds will be to discuss recommended capital improvements, emergency repairs not provided for in the annual budget, and extraordinary budget expenditures. It should go without saying that the necessary homework and advance notice ought to be a regular expectation and standard of performance for every departmental function. Do make sure that one of your best and most experienced board members serves as chairperson of this basic committee, and do trust the committee to get on with the job by authorizing them to work on their own within the limits of their position description. Nothing will stop achievement faster than having to wait for a vote of the board to buy a box of nails!

Nothing grows without cultivation, and this is especially true with respect to memorials and bequests. Most people do not think about the needs of the church by themselves. Behind every memorial or bequest at your church you will discover a personal influence. While this may or may not be something your Rector does (perhaps in his spare time), additions to your capital must be carefully planned. Otherwise, you may end up using a gold memorial chalice with a silver paten! Your memorial and bequests chairman and his committee will see to it that any new furnishings are appropriate. Further, such a group will encourage gifts to meet specific needs. Again this function could be incorporated with buildings and grounds, provided it is really necessary and there is a strong number two person on the committee.

One of the single gravest weaknesses in almost every reorganization scheme we have seen in the church has to do with follow-through. Time and time again we have observed first hand the introduction of new structures that were expected to be self-correcting. If you take the time and effort to develop position descriptions, you must make sure attention is given to their maintenance and overhaul. Your personnel chairman and his committee are charged with such a job. They are the oil for the machine, and it is their special function to keep the entire system operating smoothly and effectively. Do not skip over this function or combine it with another. We know of one congregation that adopted the two-departmental structure without a personnel function and reverted within a year to its old and tired ways. They had no procedure for making adjustments, so when difficulties were encountered they simply abandoned their agreed upon scheme for working more effectively together and insisted that the Rector and Wardens take over. This need not have happened, but there was no one whose function it was to provide for maintenance and improvement. You can avoid such a setback in your church by making sure someone is in charge of a continuing review and evaluation function.

In many congregations the Secretary or Clerk is either already an officer of the church corporation or is quickly appointed as one. Even though this is often the case, the secretary's function is really more similar in scope to that of other committee chairmen than it is to that of the officers. Accordingly we include the record-keeping function in the Administrative Department. Note also the importance of your Secretary or Clerk making copies of minutes available promptly. Nothing is so useless as dated records. Ideally minutes should be produced the day following the meeting, but especially in small churches such a standard is unrealistic. Still, you should agree on a definite delivery date. To allow a Secretary unlimited latitude in preparing minutes whenever it is convenient is really quite irresponsible. Again smaller churches might take note of a frequent practice in larger churches of appointing the paid parish secretary to assist the official Clerk by taking and transcribing minutes.

This of course enables the Clerk to participate more fully in meetings, and if your church has a member who has good shorthand and typing skills, why not consider recruiting an Assistant to the Secretary?

Perhaps there is no committee assignment where it is more important to select a chairman whose actions match his words and whose application of time and money follows a Christian commitment than in the area of stewardship. Your stewardship Chairman must practice personally what he preaches publicly. Without a personal standard of tithing or at least proportional giving of time and money, a stewardship leader really has very little to offer. Such a way of life is grounded in a personal commitment to Jesus Christ as Lord and Savior, so not only will you want a truly consecrated member of your Vestry to serve as stewardship chairman, you will find it necessary to give him or her a teaching responsibility. Every congregation must learn that the Christian does not have a choice as to whether or not to be a steward, and the most effective way this can be taught is by personal example, starting with the Rector and continuing through the stewardship chairman into the entire Vestry and congregation.

Although your clergyman has a certain amount of experience in Christian education by virtue of his seminary training, it is not his sole function to be a director of religious education. Indeed your spiritual leader needs able assistance in the development and maintenance of an all-age Christian education program for your entire congregation. Make sure there is good program co-ordination here by having a member of your church board directly accountable for this extremely important area of parish life. A Sunday School that runs itself invariably runs down! Avoid misunderstandings in your educational programs through a board level chairman who is charged with primary responsibility for all your church's Christian education efforts.

No church exists as an isolated social system devoid of community relationships. Indeed, the social implications of the Gospel compel community action. This state of affairs is worth including in your organizational chart and requires a community relations chairman. If your clergyman is the only member of your board who has an impact on the life of your community, then your membership is in effect abdicating a significant part of its ministry. To many people your church will be evaluated in terms of its total contribution to the community, so make sure this chairman has real vision for the possibilities of Christian service in your town. In a very real sense your community relations chairman is on the cutting edge of your church's mission.

There has been an increasing interest and willingness in co-operation between various religious communities and congregations. Such an ecumenical spirit in the modern era really only dates back to the Edinburgh Conference on world missions held in 1910, but it has only been since the early 1960's and Vatican II that organizational barriers to significant interdenominational ministry have begun to crumble. If ecumenical relations in your congregation are to be a vital part of your parish program in the years ahead, there must be an awareness of and a response to the fact that your spiritual leader himself cannot be a one man ecumenical committee. Do give the ecumenical function the place it deserves in your local church structure by providing a board level position for its implementation. After all, we are reminded by the late William Temple, Archbishop of Canterbury, that the divisions in Christendom are the single greatest travesty of the Gospel of Jesus Christ. Practice the biblical doctrine of the oneness of the Body of Christ by encouraging and supporting a concerted program of involvement and participation of your entire congregation with neighboring churches, temples, and religious communities.

Evangelism is to your program department what stewardship is to your administrative department. The former has to do with the birth of a Christian, and the latter has to do with his growth. One function complements the other, and so just as you need a member of your board who is personally committed to Jesus Christ and practices proportional giving as chairman of your stewardship committee, you also must have a consecrated, witnessing Christian as your evangelism chairman. His function will center chiefly on enabling the entire congregation to share the good news of what the Lord Jesus is doing in their individual lives. Needless to say, such a position will require a great deal of sensitivity to peoples' feelings, as well as a keen desire to proclaim the good news to the whole of creation.

Your fellowship chairman is intended to serve as more than a mere social director. His function is to be the main communicator and co-ordinator of all the various activities and programs sponsored by your church. This means you will want to make sure that as many people as possible have easy and direct access to the fellowship committee. Nothing is more debilitating than a parish group, eager to pursue a program, who are put off because they cannot confirm use of the church hall. Larger congregations usually assign such a scheduling task to their parish secretary; however, regardless of your church's size there should be board level oversight of fellowship programming.

Just as memorials and bequests do not usually appear all by themselves, so too formal membership does not simply take care of itself. Any congregation requires a committee with board leadership that will seek out, secure, and orient new members to participate in its life and ministry. Do not make the mistake of confusing evangelism with membership. The former is a function primarily intended for the benefit of the individual, while the latter is carried out for the sake of the local corporate Body of Christ. Your membership chairman will want to make sure there is a standard procedural pattern followed for all newcomers. Such a norm would include referrals to various church organizations, personal visitations by clergy *and* laity, and an invitation of formal membership, as well as a ninety-day review of a new member's integration into the life of the congregation. If you want increased membership, your board will have to give it serious attention, which can be quite successfully accomplished through an active membership function within your program department.

No chairman is more visible to the entire congregation than the one who is responsible for worship. In most denominations the pastor is in charge of worship; however, this does not mean help is not required or appreciated. No one person can attend to all the details necessary for a well organized service. Indeed there is no other church activity that continually demands so much time and effort from so many. Consequently, a worship chairman can be an invaluable asset by orchestrating the many parts of public worship and by enabling the ordained minister to concentrate on his specific liturgical duties. In all circumstances this committee should work closely with the pastor in order to avoid any misunderstandings or sense of competition. A strong collaborative worship group will enhance the quality of services greatly, whereas a token committee will bog your spiritual leader down in a seemingly endless series of details better managed by members of the congregation. Remember, however, that worship is the peculiar obligation of your clergyman. So make sure your worship committee works with him and not for him. Together they will make beautiful music!

CHAPTER FIVE:

Your Church Organization's Supporting Staff

If it makes sense to work out detailed position descriptions for the paid and volunteer members of your church board, it is an equally good idea to apply this same standard to other paid and volunteer staff who support your congregation's day to day operation. Written statements of expectations reflect one very thorough way to achieve an effective local church administration that is successful in direct proportion to the consistency of its application. It is not very helpful, for instance, to have a precise agreement as to the function of the worship committee and at the same time to allow people working in areas for which the worship committee is accountable to do as they please. We have found that a style of church organization based on position descriptions is only as strong as the written statement designed for the smallest functioning unit. If a part of the system operates without written, agreed-upon standards, or fails to maintain them or keep them current, sooner or later the entire system's performance will be seriously affected. All this is to say that your work is not done when you have documented board accountability. Indeed, to do position descriptions for your top leadership is to commit yourself to doing the same thing for those on whom your board relies for day-to-day support. Do not attempt only half the job. It is beter not to start than never to finish, and *your church will not possess a complete package of position descriptions until it includes both paid and volunteer staff assignments.* Curiously, many churches seem to back into such a package by starting with written agreements for their paid people.

Yet no matter where your church begins, you will find Appendix IV (pages 113–124) helpful, with its samples of some staff and volunteer position descriptions.

Obviously a difference exists between the paid staff member and the volunteer, but it is not as great as you might think. Everyone gets something for their work, from dollars to a sense of personal achievement and satisfaction. Do not try to squeeze the last drop of work out of a church employee in order to get your money's worth, and never expect a volunteer to do a continuing job without some written procedure. Avoid the trap of thinking that a salary makes the difference in performance. It does not, but sharply defined expectations and instructions can and often do. No church could continue without the untold number of volunteer hours given to it, so it is important not to abuse this invaluable asset by demanding unlimited and unstructured performance. The Vestry that treats volunteers in a business-like manner will get the results that often elude boards that act as if members of the congregation owe the church their time.

Sooner or later your board will most likely have to deal with the issue of employing a church member or an outsider. We cannot recommend to your personnel committee that it is better always to go with the non-member, nor can we advise your people to give members first consideration. It really is not too important, provided there is a detailed position description by which performance can be assessed. You can look to your personnel committee for guidance on this issue, and it would be reasonable to expect them to present to the board a policy statement on hiring practices based on an agreed upon statement of purpose. There are advantages and disadvantages in engaging both members and non-members for salaried positions. Yet in the long run you will find other factors to be much more to the point, such as actual performance, which can always be evaluated in terms of specified objectives and expectations. So let's briefly consider some staff and volunteer position descriptions.

STAFF AND VOLUNTEER CONCEPTS

Unless you want your clergyman to spend a great deal of his time doing office work, it is a good idea to employ a church secretary. Many congregations require only a part-time person, but it is the exceptional parish that can operate a church office on a strictly volunteer basis without in effect requiring the Rector to serve as an office manager. It really is a matter of priorities and whether or not your board wants to make the most of your spiritual leader's training. Many large churches with multiple-clergy staffs have found that it is often better to engage a church secretary or business manager than to fill a clergy vacancy. The point is that a certain level of administrative support is required for effective spiritual leadership, and whether this is expected of the Rector or of a church secretary is really a matter deserving the most careful consideration. In many cases a congregation might be better off to employ a part-time secretary with the necessary training and skills and a part-time pastor who is engaged for certain pastoral specialties, than it would be simply to retain a clergyman who is expected to perform in administrative areas for which he has had little training and experience. Churches would not think of hiring an organist who could not play an organ, but they would engage a pastor who could not type and then not provide a church secretary. At the very least it is a poor dollar investment to expect the clergyman to do two jobs for one of which he has no real skill, and at the most such a situation is contrary to the Word of God in expecting the eye of the body to do double duty as an ear. The position of church secretary is a distinct function and merits recognition as such with a written statement of responsibilities.

In smaller congregations the function of bookkeeper-accountant is often included in the position of treasurer. Yet there is a point, when a church reaches an annual budget of around $100,000, that it becomes unrealistic to expect volunteer time and talent to do all that is required. Very few parishes retain a full-time bookkeeper unless their payrolls include at least 25 salaried full-time personnel. For the great majority of congregations retaining an outside accountant to perform auditing responsibilities might be all that can be done. Nevertheless, it is important to be aware of the very real fiscal support your treasurer needs and to provide as much paid and volunteer help as possible. Just as your pastor needs secretarial assistance to be effective, so your treasurer should not be expected to do everything alone.

Perhaps no staff position requires greater definition than that of custodian, janitor, or sexton. Without clear lines of authority and accountability, everyone will think it perfectly proper to ask the custodian to do this, that, or the other thing. Moreover, people all too quickly get ideas not only about what should be cleaned but about how it should be done as well. After all, everyone does some domestic cleaning once in a while, and thereby thinks he or she is qualified to supervise commercial maintenance. Above all, make sure your congregation understands exactly to whom the janitor is to report, and then make sure that he politely ignores all his other would-be bosses. Under most circumstances you will find it more satisfactory to view your custodian as a maintenance contractor with whom your board has a specific written agreement for certain responsibilities at an agreed level of compensation. Generally speaking, an hourly rate is more expensive except for one-time-only projects. Some congregations attempt to have their maintenance dollar do double work as an outreach dollar as well by providing a job for a needy person within the community. While this is certainly most commendable, such a practice is questionable especially when the employee has little knowledge or experience. With a well done position description, however, it can be done quite successfully. Your buildings and grounds committee must be closely involved in developing and maintaining your custodian's written schedule of actual cleaning responsibilities.

With the obvious exception of other clergy staff, the organist and choirmaster has the closest relationship to your pastor in terms of liturgics. Organist and Rector function on a peer level when it comes to planning and actually conducting worship services. They are a unique partnership within the local church team by virtue of their training and interest in liturgy. Just as the church secretary maximizes the pastor's effectiveness through administrative support, so too the organist and choirmaster optimizes the clergyman's liturgical ministry through music from the organ and the choir. The organist is really an extension of the Rector's office, and consequently your board should treat both functions similarly. If your pastor receives a salary, so too should your organist. If your clergyman receives an increase, so too should your organist. After all, both these positions require talents and skills beyond the competence of most lay people, and as St. Paul reminds us, "The worker deserves his pay" (I Timothy 5:18).

In Appendix IV you will find five other sample position descriptions for volunteers (pages 113–124). Each statement, as with all the others in Appendix III and IV, specifies four basic items:

1. name or title of position;
2. name or title of position of person to whom accountable;
3. general statement of function;
4. list of individual responsibilities.

None of the volunteer position descriptions spells out precise procedures, since this is a matter which will vary considerably; however, you should be aware of the existence of very excellent manuals in all five areas listed here. Any church publishing house has a catalogue available on request, which lists helpful little books, such as Dorothy Diggs's *A Working Manual For Altar Guilds*, which is published by Morehouse-Barlow. Generally speaking, if you seek, you will find a written guide for almost any volunteer function in your congregation. We would suggest you include appropriate excerpts from these guides in your own position descriptions, so that it will not be necessary to reinvent the wheel every time there is a turnover in volunteers. If a position is once documented and then kept current with changes, additions and deletions, effective continuity of function will be greatly enhanced.

Young men and women who assist at the altar during services are not doing the clergyman a favor by their presence. Each congregation has certain agreed-upon standards for this position, and in fulfilling specified requirements a young person is in fact exercising a ministry of his or her own. This means acting appropriately and responsibly. A volunteer position needs as much definition as a salaried one for real effectiveness. To be absent, tardy, or unprepared is inexcusable for anyone who shares in local church ministry regardless of position, because the whole is directly affected by its parts.

In almost every congregation you see a small group of faithful and devoted women (and, in an encouraging modern trend, occasional men) who lovingly attend to the altar and its various appointments. These people are invaluable volunteer members of the local church team. Their contribution of time and talent really defies quantitative measurement in terms of dollars. Although they certainly do experience real fellowship one with another, their primary function is not a social one; rather it is a consecrated one to the greater glory of God. A detailed position description will be a great help in avoiding misunderstandings about responsibilities.

Depending on the size of your parish you will surely have either a paid or volunteer church school director or superintendent. This is a position with extremely wide scope and requires a person of real maturity. Sometimes in smaller

congregations the Rector ends up filling this position himself, which can be acceptable provided there is general
agreement. If your church school leader is a volunteer,
please do him or her the favor of specifying a term of service. It is really quite debilitating to use a volunteer until he
drops in his tracks, and perhaps no other volunteer position
ages one so quickly as that of head of the church school. So
get your Christian education committee to establish a
length-of-service standard for the good of the individual and
the parish as a whole.

Lay reading is a separate ministry all its own in the Episcopal Church. There is even a special national canon which
spells out the necessary requirements for this position.
Surely every one of your lay readers should be familiar with
these formal standards. In addition, your parish undoubtedly has some local customs and practices which should also
be specified and known. Some congregations, for instance,
have lay readers who are licensed by the Ordinary to administer the chalice under the direction of the local pres-
byter, while some parishes reserve this function for ordained
ministers. No matter what your church's practice, if it is
worth doing, it is worth documenting, so that everything
may be done decently and in order.

Ushers fulfill a volunteer function at worship as important
as that of any other staff or volunteer members of the local
church ministry team. Except in very small congregations,
visitors come in contact with the ushers first, and their manner will do much toward integrating newcomers and guests
into the service and the church. Ushers have a freedom of
movement during the service which requires the greatest
sensitivity, so encourage your head usher to recruit the best
people possible. A beginning ministry as an usher on Sundays can lead to a more extensive ministry, perhaps on the
board. You can help volunteers get a good start as ushers
by providing them with position descriptions, and thus setting a tone and a standard for the future.

CHAPTER SIX:

Local Church Organization In Action

Position descriptions by themselves, no matter how thoroughly maintained, will not make for an effective local church administration. Your congregation's effectiveness will be measured in terms of results, not organizational charts and written statements of accountability. The basic function of your board is to determine the purpose and policy by which its results can be evaluated, and in order to do this we believe it is necessary for board members, staff, and volunteers to work from interrelated written agreements of responsibility. So position descriptions are an extremely important and often neglected means to the ends for which a Church exists; however, they are by no account all that is required. There is in fact a variety of considerations which go into a dynamic and effective church organization in addition to the one that has been our central concern here. In this chapter we will explore some of these other considerations and share some of the things we have learned in that area of local church life which would be assigned to the administrative department.

BUDGET AND FINANCE

Your church's operating budget is a statement of position on forecasted and received income and on forecasted and disbursed expenditures during a stated period of time, usually a year, although analysis is more frequent. Most congregations operate a budget in twelve parts, acting as if receipts and disbursements should be uniform from month to month. This is not the case. Surely you are aware that your parish receives more income at Christmas and Easter than it does in July and August, unless your church is located in a Summer resort area. Most congregations also incur greater expenses during Winter months. So why operate an easy-to-figure budget that does not really work, when with just a little effort you can develop and maintain an operating budget that accurately reflects receipts and disbursements throughout the year? Simply review the last several years of actual monthly income and expenses to determine a percentage factor for each line-item for each month or quarter. The advantage of such a weighted budget is that at any time during the year the entire congregation can be alerted as to the actual fiscal situation.

Some people find it rather strange that churches year after year plan to spend money before it has been received. "How can money be spent that is not on hand?" So the question goes, and the answer is, "on faith." Clearly the operating budget process in most churches is a good example of structure being a function of purpose. It might very well be easier simply to assess every member a fixed fee to provide for all expenses, but such a dues structure is more appropriate to a club than to a church which professes belief in a God who knows all our needs. This does not mean a congregation should be fiscally irresponsible. Indeed, most denominations will not permit local churches to be lax in their finances. Still, voluntary financial support allows for individual responsiveness to God in a way which is circumvented by any "tax" structure.

Even though your membership approves the budget at its annual meeting, the actual control and implementation of it is one of your board's responsibilities. In order to act effectively on this, it is necessary to insure proper entry in all budget categories. For instance, to include postage expense on the office disbursement line is to restrict legitimate office expenses unduly. Again a concise written list of what items are to be considered parts of what lines can do much

to eliminate confusion and misunderstanding. Your parish
can avoid careless application of figures in the budget by
encouraging and supporting your budget and finance committee's efforts to document practices and procedures thoroughly.

In the preparation of your annual budget there should
never be any hesitancy in involving as many people as possible. You will certainly want to include the staff and officers
or representatives from all your church organizations. Moreover, you will want to begin your budget preparations well
before September, when your every-member-canvass program begins. Whether or not you do a pre-budget visitation,
it is wise to know in general what to anticipate in the next
year in terms of budget requirements. Too often the proposed operating budget is seen for the first time by the
voting members at the annual meeting. This is hardly the
way to stimulate real support. Budget planning sessions
should be open to members of the congregation with closed
executive meetings being the exception rather than the rule.

In parish finances it is characteristic and understandable
for each church group to operate its own treasury, complete
with savings and checking accounts. Such groups usually
give back to the church from their surplus. Obviously, people want to have some control over what they perceive as
their own money. Yet God is really the only capitalist. We
are all simply stewards, and there is a real question of good
stewardship when there is such a decentralized fiscal situation that a truly accurate accounting is difficult to obtain.
For the left hand to be in the dark about what the right hand
is doing is not only counterproductive; it is a cause of un-
due competitiveness as well. Even if, like most churches,
your parish is unable to work with a centralized budget, try
to emphasize a collaborative spirit by insisting on good
communication and periodic inspection of the records of all
church organizations by members of the budget and finance
committee.

When the proposed operating budget is drafted people

assume or hope there will be sufficient income during the year to meet expenses. Most churches have no alternative to working on a cash basis, which means reserves for contingencies are usually ignored. Instead of passing the hat when the boiler finally gives up the ghost, your parish would do better to budget a modest amount each year for unexpected events and then to carry forward unused monies. In this way a reserve fund would build up over the years. Such a practice, however, would mean maintaining a separate internal account to which payment could be made according to the budget, and although this is a standard bookkeeping procedure, most treasurers like to be able to move money around, robbing Peter to pay Paul. So establish a definite policy as to just how your church will deal with emergencies. It is too late to be effective when you are caught in the middle of a crisis. Even Jesus has told us to "count the cost" (Luke 14:28 RSV) before the fact, not after.

One area of budget and finance that is seldom emphasized is frequent reporting to all members with a financial interest. We know of one congregation which dramatically improved its receipts by mailing to all its pledging members a friendly and personal monthly note which summarized the church's fiscal situation and the individual's current support. The following items were neatly listed:

1. Previous month's weighted budget of receipts
2. Previous month's actual receipts
3. Deficit or surplus in previous month's receipts
4. Previous month's weighted budget of disbursements
5. Previous month's actual disbursements
6. Deficit or surplus in disbursements
7. Your pledged support for previous month
8. Your actual support for previous month
9. Deficit or surplus in your support for previous month.

Obviously it is a lot of work to prepare such a report promptly every month, but it does produce a lot of results. If your arrears are more than desired, there is something that can be done about it. If people are kept in the picture regularly, they will respond regularly. Your budget and finance people might also establish a policy of posting complete monthly treasurer's reports on your church's inside notice board as a good secondary line of communication.

There is one other area in budget and finance which is often confused, and that is the responsibility for paying denominational obligations, such as a pledge to the diocese or the national Church, and for fund raising. Neither one of these responsibilities is intrinsically a fiscal function; nevertheless, your parish may wish to include these responsibilities in its own definition of the budget and finance function, but this should be clearly spelled out. In any event do not expect your budget and finance committee to do everything by themselves. Their function is to help in fiscal matters, not to usurp the congregation's corporate responsibility for providing the monetary means for ministry and sharing with others.

BUILDINGS & GROUNDS

One vital corollary to the function of the buildings and grounds committee has to do with proper and adequate insurance coverage, which in many instances is handled in a very haphazard manner. Above all your church must maintain coverage equivalent to current soaring replacement values. Did you know that ten churches or other religious buildings catch fire every day in this country and that 50% of these are totally destroyed, according to the National Safety Council? Churches seem to be more prone to fire than other buildings, perhaps because the church plant is often closed down during the week and fires go undetected. Make sure your church is adequately protected before you need it, and obtain the necessary expertise to guide your board. Also, consider the advantages of extended coverage, which provides protection for items, such as ordinary furniture, which are routinely excluded in standard policies.

Another consideration for your buildings and grounds committee is the development and maintenance of what is referred to in accounting terms as a "plant ledger." In this record book every capital item is coded by an identifying number, then listed by name, model, date and source of purchase, initial cost and anticipated replacement date, as well as actual location. Proper recording of this information will be of great use for your insurance purposes, and your board might be quite surprised to see listed on paper all the possessions for which they are responsible.

Good property maintenance and protection requires a regular schedule of inspection tours. Apply the odd-man-out theory here by including, on a rotating basis, volunteers from the congregation who just might spot something normally overlooked. Check such obvious places as the furnace area, as well as all passageways. Do not put up with improper storage of paints and cleaning materials. Also, you might make sure your fire-extinguishers are fully charged and properly located. Outside, you will want to be sure all approaches to church properties are free of debris and in good repair so as not to cause injuries and costly legal action. This tour should include all church buildings, especially clergy housing. We know of one parish where for 35 years no member of the congregation went past the front door of the Rectory! This certainly is unfair to the Rector and his family, as well as to the Vestry and the parish. Finally, it is important to act on the findings of your periodic tours. It is useless to determine what repairs and improvements are needed unless they are going to be effected.

With respect to daily property maintenance, your church will undoubtedly rely on the services of a custodian. The individual who performs janitorial duties conscientiously should certainly be treated fairly according to his written contract and considerately by an appreciative and thoughtful congregation. You might consider some type of recognition at Christmas in the form of a bonus, instead of assuming that different church groups will do something on their own.

Not every parish organization has the ability to provide a gift, yet they all have need of custodial services. No matter what policy your board adopts on this, make sure excellence is suitably rewarded with praise and more tangible offerings of thanks.

There are certain times in the year when there is more work to be done on buildings and grounds than can be easily managed by regular means. Sometimes temporary volunteer help will do the job, as for instance when there is a particularly heavy snowfall. At other times it is helpful to set aside a few volunteer work days when big projects, such as painting, can be tackled. Such days can also be used to do general housekeeping and cleaning, such as putting storage areas in proper order and removing what in so many cases is simply an accumulation of junk. Needless to say, co-ordination and good leadership are necessary. Work days cannot be thrown together at the last minute. Supplement regular property maintenance with volunteer work parties, which achieve real results, a sense of accomplishment, and a spirit of unity.

Your buildings and grounds committee will also have to oversee removal of previously donated capital items. Old, worn-out, and obsolete pieces of furniture and equipment are of little practical use and often take up valuable space. Decisions here must be based on the greatest sensitivity to the feelings of individuals, as well as a sharp vision of the needs of the corporate local body. Here again, a written policy statement approved by your board will go a long way towards creating a positive and reasonable approach to furnishing your church. Without such a policy for providing suitable and appropriate ecclesiastical appointments, your parish is in danger of being inundated with well-meaning offers of all sorts of useless items. You should include in your policy a procedure for using monies realized from the disposition of capital items for the acquisition of other required appointments. The point here is to anticipate potential requirements and to make the necessary policy decisions before being confronted with an actual situation.

Whether your custodian, church secretary, or buildings and grounds chairman does it, make sure a responsible person oversees the distribution *and* collection of church keys. Even in churches, or perhaps especially in churches, since they are often left open and unattended, supplies and valuables must be kept under lock and key. Many congregations find it necessary actually to change all their locks and reissue keys from time to time. If your church has to do this, avoid the necessity of repeated changes by maintaining an accurate record of who has what keys, by using keys clearly stamped "not to be duplicated," and by insisting on key return when a key-holder moves away, becomes inactive, or no longer serves in a position for which a key is needed.

At this point you might be wondering why we are going into so much minutiae, and our reason is that good property maintenance and protection is the most obvious witness to the love and care expressed by the church's membership. The former Bishop of Michigan believes that a well maintained church plant is the first of five healthy marks of a parish, and certainly a visitor's very first impression of a church is based on its appearance. Moreover, keeping the church plant in good condition provides a means by which to involve members of the congregation who might not want to think of themselves as doing anything too "religious." A work day or a paint party is an excellent way to give people a sense of ownership in their buildings and grounds, and from such a base of pride and satisfaction in a job well done, a deeper and richer spiritual life can and often does develop. So for a dynamic and active congregation, do not overlook the possibilities of congregational participation in a total buildings and grounds program. It is a very effective vehicle for God's grace.

STEWARDSHIP

Your stewardship committee is charged with one of the most challenging functions for which your board is accountable. This function is the development of a combination of attitudes and behavior, both individually and collectively, which nurture the Christian use of time, talent and possessions. Above all your stewardship people must establish an educational strategy that enables the congregation to think through clearly and to respond to the deepest implications of its acceptance of Jesus Christ as Lord and Savior. Without such an overview the stewardship function is often little more than developing a church style of fund raising. Be sure your stewardship people challenge you to reach a definitive position on what it means to be a Christian in your parish. Such a statement should suggest biblical standards of proportional giving and weekly offerings, to name but a few, and you will undoubtedly look to your spiritual leader as a resource in its preparation.

With respect to specific stewardship programs you will find that they can all be categorized by one of the following three labels:

1. indirect solicitation
2. personal visitation
3. group gatherings.

The first label applies to mail and telephone campaigns. There has always been a tendency to sell a mail solicitation short; however, there are churches where such an approach is most appropriate. This particular technique has been made available commercially by Virgil W. Hensley, Inc., Oklahoma, whose approach includes a series of co-ordinated letters. Telephone solicitations usually require all the callers to be in the same place at the same time, such as at an office which has many phone lines available on a weekday evening or a Sunday afternoon. Studies confirm that a telethon approach works by insuring that contact is made. Such an approach requires a great deal of preparation and follow-through in getting a confirmation of the verbal pledge. It is unwise, however, to use this method with new members. They need a personal visitation. We know of no better one-volume manual to help you organize an effective personal visitation program than Canon W. David Crockett's *Sound Financial Stewardship*. There really is no secret to running an every-member-visitation campaign. It just takes proper attention to step-by-step details. The third label applies to a number of efforts where the members are brought together at a special dinner, a loyalty Sunday or cottage meetings. The purpose here is to get the same message over to as many people as possible. Cottage meetings provide an informal atmosphere in which a small group of about six couples can discuss their faith and its implications frankly in terms of their day-to-day commitments as Christians. Of course, the three categories of stewardship programs can be mixed. One of the most popular hybrids is a loyalty Sunday with a mop-up visitation, even though this means callers will for the most part be visiting those people who are less than enthusiastic about the local church.

One variation of the personal visitation program which merits special mention is a year-round emphasis on stewardship through a series of lay and clergy visits designed to encourage and foster greater commitment. Such a year-round program involves major board and parish-wide support to be effective. This approach understands stewardship to be of concern to the Christian every day of the year, so visits are planned to take place throughout the year on a cyclical basis. If you attempt this type of project, you might also find it helpful to incorporate a prayer cycle, published in your weekly bulletin, as a part of your visitation schedule. This cycle systematically provides for the public recognition and remembrance in corporate prayer of every family and individual in your parish, over a period of months.

Whatever your stewardship program, the fourfold functions of planning, organizing, motivating, and controlling cannot be ignored. Special attention must be given to training, since it is the volunteers who will actually be on the front lines representing the entire Church. We have found it valuable to regard any interaction in terms of a time-line with a beginning, a middle and an ending. This is nothing new. Yet to our knowledge this threefold concept has not been widely used in the Church. Your volunteers can be trained to think in terms of their opening, the middle, when an invitation to commitment is made, and an ending or closing. Often poor results are obtained from well-meaning but poorly trained volunteers, so insist on a thorough training program for all those connected with your parish's stewardship effort and ministry.

As with many areas of church life, so too with stewardship, the question of the spiritual leader's role can be raised. Obviously your pastor must be involved, but if he is the one who actually draws up the schedule and plans, the stewardship chairman is not doing his job. You should expect example and teaching from your ordained minister. He should pracitce what he preaches, and he should be articulate in sharing with everyone the biblical and theological bases for his actions. Hopefully volunteers will learn how better to express their own personal commitment by seeing and hearing how your pastor offers his witness.

One important adjunct to the work of your stewardship committee is the development and maintenance of a complete inventory of the talents, skills, and interests of your church's membership. Such a file should include both the young and the old, and even those who are inactive in parish life. Every person associated with your parish has a particular ministry, and one of the real values of a talent bank is that it enables people to declare the nature of their vocation in terms of their talents, skills, and interests. Not only should every member of your board be assigned a specific functional responsibility, every member of your congregation should have some responsibility as well. They should all feel they have a definite part to play in the life of the parish. Since every member is a minister, it is certainly good stewardship to sort out and keep track of who is doing what. Also be sure that, once people offer their time and talent, it is put to good use. You might well imagine how disheartened is the lady who volunteered to bake cakes and then was never asked. A properly used talent inventory will produce fulfillment, not frustration.

TELEPHONE AND OFFICE DETAIL

At this point we offer some thoughts on secondary considerations which will contribute to your dynamic and effective church organization. First, there is the telephone and how it is answered. Believe it or not, even the poorest parish in this country can afford an answering service. A church cannot afford *not* to have its phone answered promptly and courteously twenty-four hours a day. It really is unfair to the pastor's family to have the church telephone ring at the parsonage, unless this is mutually agreeable. Better to engage an answering service for pennies a day, or to purchase one of the inexpensive answering tape machines, or to arrange to have the church number ring in the home of a trustworthy and competent shut-in. It is important to realize that there is no excuse for an unanswered phone. It does not matter what great help may be available in your parish if no one is available when the help is really needed. With the great distances involved in many rural and suburban parishes some clergy are even making use of citizen band radio to insure that opportunities for ministry will not be missed simply because there was no one to answer a call.

It is somewhat surprising how little the average lay person is aware of the volumes of paper that are processed in any church during a year. Standard forms can be a real aid, and such publishing houses as Morehouse-Barlow have developed a seemingly endless variety of printed materials. Just one example is the illustration of a handy parish record card on the next page. It really is unnecessary to design your own forms when such flexible items as the parish record card are so available.

More volunteer-hours are probably consumed at church meetings than at any other single activity with the possible exception of actual worship services. Consequently it is im-

FAMILY NAME		CHRISTIAN NAME		BORN	B	C	C
		WIFE'S CHRISTIAN NAME					

RESIDENCE		TELEPHONE
1		
2		
3		

OCCUPATION		BUSINESS ADDRESS	

HOW RECEIVED		FROM		YEAR		CHURCH PAPER

OTHER MEMBERS OF FAMILY

NAME	BORN	RELATION	B	C	C	OCCUPATION	BUS. ADDR. OR REMOVAL

FAMILY CARD — A PERMANENT RECORD CARD FOR PARISH FAMILIES, TO BE KEPT FILED AND SUPPLEMENTED BY ADDITIONAL CARDS IF REQUIRED. MARK CARDS CLEARLY 1, 2, 3, ETC. IF MORE THAN ONE CARD IS IN USE.

FAMILY REMOVED TO_____

YEAR_____ DATE TRANSFERRED_____

portant to make the most of meeting time. Whether the annual meeting, the monthly board or departmental meeting, a committee meeting, or a work meeting, the most effective aid is an agenda. With an agreed-upon procedure, business can be handled with dispatch, whereas without a thought-out plan there is little sense of movement or achievement. The exact order of business is unimportant, as long as there is an order accepted by the membership present at the start of the meeting. If you really want to expedite matters, publish a proposed agenda before an annual meeting, so people will know what to expect and what to suggest as changes.

In one sense this chapter has been a further elaboration of the duties of some of the administrative department's committees. Hopefully each committee will generate its own commentary in writing as it goes along. There is always a better way, but we cannot strive for increased excellence unless we know what has gone before. We cannot know what has gone before unless someone has documented previous efforts. So in addition to various collections of policies and practices, at the very least each warden should keep an informal diary of events and learnings. Over the years such papers will make it possible for succeeding generations to reach ever higher to the greater glory of God.

CHAPTER SEVEN:

Presenting Your Church By Publicity And Promotion

Far too many congregations fail to provide a promotional piece about themselves for general distribution in the community. Who can better tell other people about your parish than your own people? No matter how established a church is, a little leaflet which briefly summarizes its people, purpose, and programs will go a long way toward creating and maintaining a positive image in the community. If you leave it up to the people to seek out your parish, this can easily be misinterpreted as evidence of a lack of interest in the community. Avoid such a possible misrepresentation by producing and distributing a leaflet. It need not be fancy, but it should be neat and to the point. Make it as attractive as you can, because you will want to give it the widest possible circulation in real estate offices, shops, and wherever it can be displayed. You will also want to be sure that all members of the board and any other interested parishioners have supplies to pass out to neighbors and friends.

Another important way to present your parish to the public is through the local newspaper. Here clergy cooperation can be extremely helpful if your rector can cultivate an ongoing relationship with the religion reporter or editor. In dealing with newspapers, copy must be prompt and to the point. Deadlines must be observed strictly, and articles should be about local people in the newspaper's readership area. A good idea is to have one member of your community relations committee assigned to oversee all newspaper releases, even if they are prepared by the church secretary.

As to how to write a newspaper release, your newspaper publicity person will find it extremely valuable to make an appointment with the local religion editor in order to learn what the paper's policy requires and prefers. If your people wait to talk with local newspaper officials until there is a special story for which coverage is desired, there will be less chance of co-operation than if there is a long-standing relationship. Too often churches concentrate only on their own community's daily or weekly paper and overlook submitting the same article, in a newly typed original, to more than one newspaper. This negligence is a mistake. The policy for newspaper publicity in your community relations committee should be: "If you'll print it, we'll write it."

Did you know there are over 7,000 radio stations in this country? There are only a few industry giants, such as ABC, CBS, and NBC. Most radio stations are small and local. They have much to offer your congregation in terms of increasing community awareness of your church's ministry and program. Some stations will actually give free air time to clergy for inspirational messages, while others will charge churches only a fraction of their regular commercial rates. In any event a radio ministry is well worth serious consideration by your community relations committee as well as by your program department. Radio might seem to be a rather exotic form of communication, but a surprising statistic indicates that every home in America has an average of three radios! Again clergy initiative will be helpful in sustaining a radio program. We know of a congregation that has used the equivalent of thousands of dollars of commercial air time to broadcast its message, all without charge by virtue of the pastor's conscientiousness and consistency. Do not overlook the possibilities and potential in presenting your church over the radio, and remember that the Federal Communications Commission (F.C.C.) in Washington, D.C., requires radio stations to be responsive to the needs of the community, which includes the people in your congregation. Television might still be out of the reach of most parishes, but this certainly is not the case with radio. Think about it.

In recent years mainline Protestant denominations have produced standardized road signs so that people can easily identify their local churches. Be sure there are enough properly located signs to guide any stranger or visitor in the area to the doorsteps of your parish. Nothing is more annoying to the motorist than following the directions on a church sign to an intersection that is not clearly marked. Unlike newspaper publicity, the basic work in installing signs is a job that only needs doing once. Then it is simply a matter of a little routine maintenance, perhaps sponsored by your buildings and grounds committee. One word of caution is in order: obtain proper authorization and permits before digging your holes!

Most churches in this country produce a weekly Sunday bulletin which lists the order of service and notices for the week. This little item, so often left behind in pews and on chairs, can be an extremely effective promotional piece for your parish. Why not mail it to shut-ins and leave it with newcomers in the community? Invite members of the congregation to pass their copies of the bulletins on to family, neighbors, and friends. It is poor stewardship simply to collect the bulletins after services every week and throw them out—but do leave one for the trash man! Since this will be a herald of your church, it is important to produce a neat and attractive bulletin, perhaps with a preprinted cover with a picture of the church itself. The promotional and ministering potential of your little weekly bulletin is great, and it deserves as careful attention as any other church program.

It seems odd, but some congregations think they cannot afford to advertise in the yellow pages of their local telephone directory. It is not necessary to list the name of the pastor and the time of services, or to have a listing in bold type, but it is extremely important to insure the availability of your church's phone number to all. If you can afford a church phone, you can afford the few additional pennies to have it commercially listed. After all, you need only obtain one pledging member a year as a result of your yellow pages listing to more than justify the expense. You can easily discover for yourself how many people found your church through the yellow pages by asking newcomers. Chances are you will be surprised.

Another way to present your parish to the community is with neat and attractive posters announcing church-sponsored activities and programs. Shopping centers and stores will welcome these signs, provided Christmas events are not being advertised in July. Laundromats and other areas where the public gather to wait for services are also good areas to post church related notices from time to time. Your community relations committee should map out and keep track of where church posters are displayed.

Monthly newsletters are usually treated as if they were only for members of the congregation. This should not be the case at all. Send copies of your monthly mailing to township officials, certain civic leaders, and other congregations. Let everyone know what is going on in your parish. Again, as with the bulletin, your newsletter should be attractive. It is better not to let people know what your church is doing than to create the impression your church does not care how it looks or what it does. The ministry of the printed word is every bit as important as that of the spoken word, or pastoral and social action. Consequently it requires proper preparation and production.

If your parish has an outside notice board, be sure it is maintained, properly lighted at nights, and changed weekly. Once road signs bring newcomers to your church, an attractive outside notice board will encourage them to come in the doors. If your congregation is without such a display board, think about including one in your next year's budget. Some churches have very effective ministries through the messages posted for passing motorists. Again, effort spent in installing an outside notice board is minimal compared to the years of use your parish will receive from it in return.

One area often overlooked in terms of publicity is your church's letterhead and logo. Many denominations have national identification symbols, which may be included in your parish's image on paper; however, avoid mixing ecclesiastical graphics. We know of one Episcopal church that carries a stylized cross and flame of the United Methodist Church on its envelopes, which is somewhat confusing, to say the least. Many local churches include a design or picture distinctive to their congregation in their letterhead. Whether simple or sophisticated, your church letterhead presents a subliminal message worth serious consideration. For instance a church letter with the name of the pastor crossed out can suggest a certain unsettledness. Because of clergy mobility, with the average assignment lasting only some three years, many parishes do not include staff listings on their letterhead. This is a matter of personal taste and should be discussed. Certainly cost of printing is a factor; as a matter of fact, any congregation that uses multi-color embossed stationery is "saying" money is no obstacle. Such stationery suggests a different purpose than the servitude emphasized in the Gospel of Jesus Christ. Finally, we have found the idea of reproducing the church letterhead in miniature on a calling card for the staff very helpful. By using a folded-over card the church image can be printed on the front and the staff person's name can be set at the bottom on the inside of the back flap. This arrangement allows the card to be stood up and messages to be transmitted with some degree of privacy. The card is still usable once the staff person moves on simply by cleanly cutting off the bottom part of the back flap.

If your program people are interested in more ideas and greater detail in this area, we know of no better contemporary booklet than Canon Crockett's *Promotion And Publicity For Churches*. This is really a companion piece to *Sound Financial Stewardship*, and you will find that both volumes serve your two departments extremely well.

Postscript

"When you *assume* anything at all, it usually makes an *ASS* out of *U* and *ME!*" So spoke a shrewd senior warden to a young seminarian some years ago. If possible, we hope to avoid making an ass out of anyone by acknowledging that this little book is based on many unexplicated assumptions in the area of managerial theology. We have intended to provide you with a manual that works, and in order to do this we have glossed over interesting implications easily associated with such an objective. Nevertheless, our primary concern has been to document for you a way we have found produces a highly effective local church administration. Our basic focus has been "how," not "why." There are, however, three basic presuppositions on which our work depends. Briefly they are as follows.

First, administration is not a dirty word with respect to the essential functioning of the church. Indeed, the word "minister" is its root concept. It really is not a question of whether or not to be an administrator in the Church; rather, the question is whether one is to be an able administrator or a poor one. Clearly, good administration is no accident, and the social sciences offer us much help in understanding what is required for able administration. We believe administration is as important as any area of church life, not because it necessarily has any intrinsic value of its own, but because it represents the means by which all other avenues of ministry are traversed. We therefore would refer to this area of church life as a "metafunction" which enables the whole Church of laity and clergy to exercise God's ministry to the world.

Secondly, every Christian is called to be a minister in specific ways. This means that no one member of the clergy is more representative of the Church than any other baptized member. Of course a bishop does have certain ecclesiastical duties different from the obligations of a lay man or woman, but such a distinction in vocation in no way makes the bishop more or the lay person less personally responsible for ministry. The real issue is not one of church rank but of faithfulness to God through the Gospel of Jesus Christ. There is the fundamental obligation of all baptized members of the Church to minister in whatever way possible.

Thirdly, effective ministry by the whole Church to the whole world requires a precise definition of functions and responsibilities. We believe the Holy Spirit works through structures as well as through people. Documenting who is to do what by when for whom is one very good example of how the Holy Spirit brings people together for effective ministry. Through the development of position descriptions, for instance, people are enabled to use their special gifts with the comforting knowledge that such a structure frees other people to specialize in the offering of their talents, all of which are harmonized for the upbuilding of the Body of Christ.

We do not intend to defend these three basic presuppositions, merely to articulate them so that you will know on what we base our work and will perhaps be able to use our findings to some advantage in your own work. May our work here be of real help to you in your ministry, and may the position descriptions you write for your manual be of as much help to you as ours have been to us.

Certain Organizational Canons Of The General Church

TITLE I CANON 5

OF THE MODE OF SECURING AN ACCURATE VIEW OF THE STATE OF THIS CHURCH

Sec. 1. A report of every Parish and other Congregation of this Church shall be prepared annually for the year ending December 31st preceding, upon the blank form prepared by the Executive Council and approved by the Committee on the State of the Church, and shall be sent in duplicate not later than February 1st to the Bishop of the Diocese, or, where there is no Bishop, to the Secretary of the Diocese. The Bishop or the Secretary, as the case may be, shall send the duplicate copy to the Executive Council not later than March 1st. In every Parish the preparation and delivery of this report shall be the joint duty of the Rector and Vestry; and in every other Congregation the duty of the Minister in charge thereof.

TITLE I CANON 6

OF BUSINESS METHODS IN CHURCH AFFAIRS

Sec. 1. In every Diocese, Parish, Mission, and Institution, connected with this Church, the following standard business methods shall be observed:

(1). Trust and permanent funds and all securities of whatsoever kind shall be deposited with a Federal or State Bank, or a Diocesan Corporation, or with some other agency approved in writing by the Finance Committee or the Department of Finance of the Diocese, under either a deed of trust or an agency agreement, providing for at least two signatures on any order of withdrawal of such funds or securities.

But this paragraph shall not apply to funds and securities refused by the depositories named as being too small for acceptance. Such small funds and securities shall be under the care of the persons or corporations properly responsible for them.

(2). Records shall be made and kept of all trust and permanent funds showing at least the following:

(a) Source and date.
(b) Terms governing the use of principal and income.
(c) To whom and how often reports of condition are to be made.
(d) How the funds are invested.

(3). Treasurers and custodians, other than banking institutions, shall be adequately bonded; except treasurers of funds that do not exceed five hundred dollars at any one time during the fiscal year.

(4). Books of account shall be so kept as to provide the basis for satisfactory accounting.

(5). All accounts shall be audited annually by a Certified or Independent Public Accountant, or by such an accounting agency as shall be permitted by the Finance Committee or Department of Finance of the Diocese.

A certificate of audit shall be forwarded to the Bishop or Ecclesiastical Authority not later than July 1 of each year, covering the financial reports of the previous calendar year.

(6). All buildings and their contents shall be kept adequately insured.

(7) The Finance Committee or Department of Finance of the Diocese or Missionary District may require copies of any or all accounts described in this Section to be filed with it and shall report annually to the Convention of the Diocese upon its administration of this Canon.

(8). The fiscal year shall begin January 1.

Sec. 2. The several Dioceses shall give effect to the foregoing standard business methods by the enactment of Canons appropriate thereto, which Canons shall invariably pro-

vide for a Finance Committee or a Department of Finance
of the Diocese.

Sec. 3. No Vestry, Trustee, or other body authorized by
Civil or Canon law to hold, manage, or administer real property for any Parish, Mission, Congregation, or Institution,
shall encumber or alienate the same or any part thereof
without the written consent of the Bishop and Standing
Committee of the Diocese of which the Parish, Mission,
Congregation, or Institution is a part, except under such
regulations as may be prescribed by Canon of the Diocese.

TITLE I CANON 12

OF PARISHES AND CONGREGATIONS

Sec. 1. Every Congregation of this Church shall belong to
the Church in the Diocese in which its place of worship is
situated; and no Minister having a Parish or Cure in more
than one jurisdiction shall have a seat in the Convention of
any jurisdiction other than that in which he has canonical
residence.

Sec. 2. (a). The ascertainment and defining of the boundaries of existing Parishes or Parochial Cures, as well as the
establishment of a new Parish or Congregation, and the formation of a new Parish within the limits of any other Parish,
is left to the action of the several Diocesan Conventions.

(b). Until a Canon or other regulation of a Diocesan Convention shall have been adopted, the formation of new
Parishes, or the establishment of new Parishes or Congregations within the limits of existing Parishes, shall be vested
in the Bishop of the Diocese, acting by and with the advice
and consent of the Standing Committee thereof, and, in
case of there being no Bishop, in the Ecclesiastical Authority.

Sec. 3 (a). Where Parish boundaries are not defined by
law, or settled by Diocesan Authority under Section 2 of
this Canon, or are not otherwise settled, they shall be defined by the civil divisions of the State as follows:

Parochial boundaries shall be the limits as fixed by law,
of a village, town, township, incorporated borough, city, or

of some division of any such civil district, which may be recognized by the Bishop, acting with the advice and consent of the Standing Committee, as constituting the boundaries of a Parish.

(b). If there be but one Church or Congregation within the limits of such village, town, township, borough, city, or such division of a civil district, as herein provided, the same shall be deemed the Parochial Cure of the Minister having charge thereof. If there be two or more Churches or Congregations therein, it shall be deemed the Cure of the Ministers thereof.

(c). This Canon shall not affect the legal rights of property of any Parish or Congregation.

TITLE I CANON 13

OF PARISH VESTRIES

Sec. 1. In every Parish of this Church the number, mode of election, and term of office of Wardens and Vestrymen, with the qualifications of voters, shall be such as the State or Diocesan law may permit or require, and the Wardens and Vestrymen elected under such law shall hold office until their successors are elected and have qualified.

Sec. 2. Except as provided by the law of the State or of the Diocese, the Vestry shall be agents and legal representatives of the Parish in all matters concerning its corporate property and the relations of the Parish to its Clergy.

Sec. 3. Unless it conflict with the law as aforesaid, the Rector, when present shall preside in all the meetings of the Vestry.

TITLE I CANON 16

OF REGULATIONS RESPECTING THE LAITY

Sec. 1. All persons who have received the Sacrament of Holy Baptism with water in the name of the Father, and of the Son, and of the Holy Ghost, and whose baptism has been duly recorded in this Church, are members thereof.

Sec. 2. All baptized persons who shall for one year next preceding have fulfilled the requirements of the Canon "Of the Due Celebration of Sundays," unless for good cause prevented, are members of this Church in good standing.

Sec. 3. All such members in good standing who have been confirmed by a Bishop of this Church or a Bishop of a Church in communion with this Church or have been received into this Church by a Bishop of this Church, and who shall, unless for good cause prevented, have received Holy Communion at least thrice during the next preceding year, are communicants in good standing.

Sec. 4. Every communicant or baptized member of this Church shall be entitled to equal rights and status in any Parish or Mission thereof. He shall not be excluded from the worship or Sacraments of the Church, nor from parochial membership, because of race, color, or ethnic origin.

Sec. 5 (a). A communicant or baptized member in good standing, removing from one Parish or Congregation to another, shall be entitled to receive and shall procure from the Rector or Minister of the Parish or Congregation of his or her last enrollment or, if there be no Rector or Minister, from one of the Wardens, a certificate addressed to the Rector or Minister of the Parish or Congregation to which removal is desired, stating that he or she is duly registered or enrolled as a communicant or baptized member in the Parish or Congregation from which he or she desires to be transferred, and the Rector or Minister or Warden of the Parish or Congregation to which such communicant or baptized member may remove shall enroll him or her as a communicant or baptized member when such certificate is presented, or, on failure to produce such certificate through no fault of such communicant or baptized member, upon other evidence of his or her being such a communicant or baptized member, sufficient in the judgment of said Rector or Minister. Notice of such enrollment in such Parish or Congregation to which such communicant or baptized member shall have removed shall be sent by the Rector or

Minister thereof to the Rector of the Parish from which the communicant or baptized member is removed.

(b). Any communicant of any Church in communion with this Church shall be entitled to the benefit of this Section so far as the same can be made applicable.

(c). It shall be the duty of the Rector or Minister of every Parish or Congregation, learning of the removal of any member of his Parish or Congregation to another Cure without having secured a letter of transfer, as herein provided, to transmit to the Minister of such Cure a letter of advice informing him thereof.

Sec. 6. When a person to whom the Sacraments of the Church shall have been refused, or who has been repelled from the Holy Communion under the Rubrics, or who desires a judgment as to his status in the Church, shall lodge a complaint or application with the Bishop, or Ecclesiastical Authority, it shall be the duty of the Bishop, or Ecclesiastical Authority, unless he or it sees fit to require the person to be admitted or restored because of the insufficiency of the cause assigned by the Minister, to institute such an inquiry as may be directed by the Canons of the Diocese or Missionary District, and should no such Canon exist, the Bishop or Ecclesiastical Authority shall proceed according to such principles of law and equity as will insure an impartial decision; but no Minister of this Church shall be required to admit to the Sacraments a person so refused or repelled, without the written direction of the Bishop or Ecclesiastical Authority.

TITLE II CANON 1

OF THE DUE CELEBRATION OF SUNDAYS

All persons within this Church shall celebrate and keep the Lord's Day, commonly called Sunday, by regular participation in the public worship of the Church, by hearing the Word of God read and taught, and by other acts of devotion and works of charity, using all godly and sober conversation.

Some New Jersey Statutes As Examples of Civil Laws

TITLE 16, "CORPORATIONS AND ASSOCIATIONS, RELIGIOUS"

16:12-8 MEETINGS OF VESTRY.

Meetings of the vestry shall be called on at least twenty-four hours' notice by:

a. The rector at any time;

b. The wardens, if there is no rector, or if the rector is absent from the diocese for three calendar months, or is incapable of acting, or if the rector has refused to call the meeting within one week after the receipt of a request signed by a majority of the members of the vestry; or

c. A majority of the members of the vestry, in case of failure of the wardens to call such meeting within one week after the receipt of such request.

16:12-9 VESTRY; QUORUM.

To constitute a quorum of the vestry there must be present either:

a. The rector, one of the wardens and a majority of the vestrymen; or

b. The rector, both wardens and one less than a majority of the vestrymen; or

c. The rector and two-thirds of the vestrymen; or

d. If the rector is absent from the diocese, or is incapable of acting, and shall have been so absent or incapable for more than three calendar months, or if the meeting is called by the rector and he is absent therefrom, or if the meeting is called by the wardens or vestrymen and the rector is absent therefrom, one warden and a majority of the vestry-men, or both wardens and one less than a majority of the vestrymen.

If there is a rector called to or settled in the parish, no action shall be taken in his absence relating to or affecting the personal or exclusive rights of the rector, or the aliena-tion of the capital or principal of any investments held by the corporation, or the sale of its real estate, or the encum-brance thereof, except as may be necessary for ordinary repairs.

16:12-11 ELECTION OF OFFICERS; TENURE.

At each annual election of any such parish incorporated after March twentieth, one thousand nine hundred and one, one warden shall be elected to hold office for two years, or until his successor is chosen, and one-third of the total num-ber of vestrymen shall be elected to hold office for three years, or until their successors are chosen, and of any such parish incorporated prior to March twentieth, one thousand nine hundred and one, both wardens and all the vestrymen may be elected to hold office for one year, or until their suc-cessors are chosen, or one warden shall be elected to hold office for two years, or until his successor is chosen, and one-third of the total number of vestrymen shall be elected to hold office for three years, or until their successors are chosen, notwithstanding any provisions in the charters or certificates of incorporation of any such parishes, congrega-tions, societies or churches.

Sample Position Descriptions

Position:	**RECTOR, VICAR, OR MINISTER-IN-CHARGE**
Reports to:	**THE BISHOP OR DESIGNATED ECCLESIASTICAL SUPERIOR**
Function:	**PROVIDES FOR THE OVERALL DEVELOPMENT AND SPIRITUAL GROWTH OF THE CONGREGATION**

Responsibilities:

1. Applies emphasis on a list of no more than six pastoral specialties mutually agreed upon with the Vestry or Executive Committee following recommendations of the Personnel Committee using the following list of program areas:

TEACHER-CHILDREN, ability to teach and work with pre-teenage children;

YOUTH WORKER-TEACHER, ability to teach and work with youth within the realm of their own interests;

TEACHER-ADULTS, ability to teach and lead discussion and forum groups with adults;

VISITOR-HOMES, interest in visiting church members in their homes;

VISITOR-CRISIS, interest in visiting people in the midst of crisis, e.g., death, sickness, birth, trauma, success or other significant points in individual lives;

COUNSELOR, ability in a formal counseling setting to assist persons facing problems or decisions;

ADMINISTRATIVE LEADER, ability to manager the affairs of the congregation organization;

EVANGELISM LEADER, interest in relating the Christian faith to persons outside the church and in enabling lay leaders to bear personal witness;

INTER-CHURCH COOPERATION, interest in programs sponsored inter-denominationally or jointly by a number of churches;

SOCIAL MINISTRY LEADER, ability to enable persons within the congregation to become aware of and participate in issues;

COMMUNITY LEADER, ability through personal involvement to organize community groups to meet stated needs such as drug problems, fair housing, and school issues;

STEWARDSHIP LEADER, ability to lead lay persons in the development and use of individual and congregational resources;

THEOLOGIAN, ability to communicate a comprehensive understanding of the Bible and Christian theology;

PUBLIC SPEAKER, ability to speak with clarity and to make the Gospel relevant to people's lives, e.g., preaching;

WORSHIP LEADER, ability to plan and conduct public worship;

MINISTER OF SACRAMENTS/ORDINANCES, ability to help persons relate to the Gospel through formal/liturgical ordinances.

2. As a PASTOR, sensitizes himself to the feelings and needs of the congregation, attempting to facilitate understanding and communication at and between all levels, responding appropriately as required.

3. As a PRIEST licensed or canonically resident in a particular ecclesiastical jurisdiction or diocese, participates appropriately at a district, synodical, provincial, national, and/or international level with the advice and consent of the local governing body.

4. As a PROPHET, addresses himself to situations contrary to the Word of God in the context of the doctrine, discipline, and worship of his particular denomination both publicly and privately.

5. As a PERSON, makes available appropriate time for his own personal needs and those of his family, to include a mutually agreed upon amount of time off per week, as well as the number of annual vacation/sick days.

6. As a PROFESSIONAL, participates in an annual review process which includes evaluation of performance and identification of goals, objectives, and procedures.

7. As an EX-OFFICIO MEMBER, of all organizations and groups within the congregation, serves and participates as required.

8. As the PRESIDING OFFICER, conducts the Annual Meeting and the monthly meetings of the Vestry or Executive Committee; prepares all necessary reports as per canons and State statutes and participates in requested studies and surveys.

9. Meets with the Personnel Committee whenever there is a matter of concern about the parish-pastor relationship.

10. Supervises all paid and volunteer staff and assists in development of necessary personnel policies.

11. Provides for a periodic review and update of this description incorporating and/or deleting responsibilities mutually agreed upon as required.

12. Delegates responsibilities appropriately while maintaining overall accountability; recruits necessary personnel for effective performance of function.

Position:	**WARDEN AND ADMINISTRATIVE DEPARTMENT CHAIRMAN**
Reports to:	**RECTOR**
Function:	**DEVELOPS AND MAINTAINS ADEQUATE CONTROLS, RECORDS, AND ADMINISTRATION TO INSURE EFFECTIVE OPERATION AND UTILIZATION OF CONGREGATIONAL RESOURCES**

Responsibilities:

1. In consultation with officers appoints members of the Vestry or Executive Committee to chair the following areas for a minimum period of one year:

   a. Budget and Finance

   b. Buildings and Grounds

   c. Fund Raising

   d. Memorials and Bequests

   e. Personnel

   f. Secretary or Clerk

   g. Stewardship.

2. Ascertains that each Chairman selects adequate and qualified members for his committee by recruiting from the membership of the entire congregation.

3. Assists each of his Chairmen in updating and reviewing their position descriptions prior to Annual Meeting.

4. Chairs at least one meeting of his Department each month or as otherwise required.

5. Requires adequate reports, written or verbal, from each Chairman monthly or as otherwise agreed upon.

6. Serves ex-officio on all his Department's committees and attends meetings as required.

7. Summarizes and reports to the Vestry or Executive Committee on departmental progress and requests, calling upon his Chairmen for presentations as required.

8. Cooperates with other officers in areas where functions overlap or are unclear, and meets regularly with them for the purposes of planning and evaluating.

9. In the absence of the Rector or Vicar, assumes temporary authority for all functions and responsibilities on an equal basis with the Warden and Chairman of the Program Department.

10. Sets an example for the congregation in his public and private prayer life.

11. Delegates responsibilities appropriately while maintaining overall accountability for his function; recruits necessary personnel for effective performance.

Position:	**WARDEN AND PROGRAM DEPARTMENT CHAIRMAN**
Reports to:	**RECTOR**
Function:	**DEVELOPS AND MAINTAINS LONG RANGE GOALS, PLANS, AND PROGRAMS OF THE CONGREGATION WITH QUARTERLY EVALUATIONS AND REVIEWS OF EFFECTIVENESS**

Responsibilities:

1. In consultation with officers appoints members of the Vestry or Executive Committee to chair the following areas for a minimum period of one year:

   a. Christian Education
   b. Community Relations
   c. Ecumenical Relations
   d. Evangelism
   e. Fellowship
   f. Membership
   g. Worship

2. Ascertains that each Chairman selects adequate and qualified members for his committee by recruiting from the membership of the entire congregation.

3. Assists each of his Chairmen in updating and reviewing their position descriptions prior to Annual Meeting.

4. Chairs at least one meeting of his Department each month or as otherwise required.

5. Requires adequate reports, written or verbal, from each Chairman monthly or as otherwise agreed upon.

6. Serves ex-officio on all his Department's committees and attends meetings as required.

7. Summarizes and reports to the Vestry or Executive Committee on departmental progress and requests calling upon his Chairmen for presentations as required.

8. Cooperates with other officers in areas where functions overlap or are unclear, and meets regularly with them for the purposes of planning and evaluating.

9. In the absence of the Rector or Vicar, assumes temporary authority for all functions and responsibilities on an equal basis with the Warden and Chairman of the Administrative Department.

10. Sets an example for the congregation in his public and private prayer life.

11. Delegates responsibilities appropriately while maintaining overall accountability for his function; recruits necessary personnel for effective performance.

Position:	**TREASURER**
Reports to:	**RECTOR**
Function:	**PROVIDES OVERALL CONTROL OF RE-CEIPTS, DISBURSEMENTS, ACCOUNTS, AND RECORDS OF ALL CONGREGA-TIONAL FUNDS**

Responsibilities:

1. In consultation with officers, appoints Assistant Treasurers to the following areas for a minimum period of one year:

a. Receipts and Deposits

b. Pledge Records.

2. Insures procedures to collect and deposit all funds immediately on receipt.

3. Insures pledge payment records are properly maintained and distributed at least quarterly.

4. Accounts to the Vestry or Executive Committee for all categories of receipts and disbursements.

5. Reports monthly in writing on receipts, disbursements and their relationship to amounts budgeted.

6. Pays all salaries and bills as they fall due as follows:

a. Salaries, utilities, mortgages, and disciplinary obligations, such as an assessment, are to be paid monthly or as otherwise scheduled;

b. All other bills are to be paid as approved by Committee Chairmen or properly authorized persons.

7. Insures that all checks are countersigned by the Rector or one of the Wardens.

8. Transfers all funds received for special purposes to proper savings accounts or disburses to specified outside beneficiaries.

9. Maintains checking and savings accounts and verifies balances as statements are received.

10. Confers with Budget and Finance Chairman on changes in structure as required.

11. Maintains a record of all mortgage payments and keeps an up-to-date balance on all loans.

12. Keeps all accounting procedures up-to-date and makes necessary records available for the annual outside audit.

13. Serves as a member of the Vestry or Executive Committee, a member of the Budget and Finance Committee and an officer of the congregation.

14. Assists in preparation of annual reports as required.

15. Sets an example for the congregation in his public and private prayer life.

16. Delegates responsibilities appropriately while maintaining overall accountability for his function; recruits necessary personnel for effective performance of his duties.

Position:	**BUDGET AND FINANCE CHAIRMAN**
Reports to:	**WARDEN AND ADMINISTRATIVE DE-PARTMENT CHAIRMAN**
Function:	**MAINTAINS ADEQUATE ACCOUNTING METHODS, PROCEDURES, AND PRACTICES TO PRESENT A CONTINUOUS FINANCIAL PROFILE OF THE CONGREGATION**

Responsibilities:

1. Prepares a statement of estimated financial needs for the following year by the end of September.

2. Monitors the congregation's approved budget and offers comments on the Treasurer's monthly report with respect to differences between actual and budgeted categories and amounts.

3. Recommends budgetary exceptions, through the Administrative Department, for action by the Vestry or Executive Committee.

4. Confirms prompt payment of all salaries and bills as income provides and also insures use of tax exempt certificate for all purchases.

5. Acts as a purchasing agent in determining best source of supplies and suppliers.

6. Provides periodic reports to the congregation on indebtedness and repayment progress.

7. Determines best ways and means for protection of all investments and receipt of general gifts.

8. Insures that proper accounting procedures and controls are maintained and also provides for the annual audit.

9. Payment of disciplinary outreach, such as a quota, according to actual receipts as a percentage of the budget.

10. Assists Treasurer in insuring adequate control and guardianship of all funds prior to deposit.

11. Prepares proposed budget of the congregation for the next year in consultation with the officers.

12. Sets an example for the congregation in his public and personal prayer life.

13. Delegates responsibilities appropriately while maintaining overall accountability for his function; recruits necessary personnel for effective performance.

Position:	**BUILDINGS AND GROUNDS CHAIRMAN**
Reports to:	**WARDEN AND ADMINISTRATIVE DE-PARTMENT CHAIRMAN**
Function:	**PROVIDES MAINTENANCE AND MAN-AGEMENT OF ALL BUILDINGS AND GROUNDS OWNED BY THE CHURCH**

Responsibilities:

1. Provides adequate cleaning services for the church, through either a Sexton or an outside cleaning service, as follows:

    a. Details in writing a complete housekeeping description.

    b. Inspects cleaning performance on a weekly basis, according to a written agreement.

2. Maintains supervision of heating units and fuel supplies in the church and the parsonage.

3. Verifies electrical equipment against overloads and includes examination of wiring and outlets in inspection tours.

4. Makes a semi-annual inspection of all church properties to determine necessary repairs.

5. Sees to all repairs and purchases of supplies for the church and grounds. Expenditures to be kept within budgetary limits on a quarterly basis, with exceptions approved by the Vestry or Executive Committee.

6. Sees to all repairs of the parsonage to insure structural soundness and safety. Requests by the Rector or Vicar for additional repairs or improvements are to be reviewed by the entire Buildings and Grounds Committee.

7. Provides long range schedule of capital expenditures and replacements, additions, or improvements for consideration each year during the budget making process.

8. Sees to maintenance and upkeep of grounds at the church, which includes landscaping, mowing, trimming, fertilizing, seeding, etc. Also sees to removal of snow and ice from walks and parking areas.

9. Establishes and publishes definite procedures for all volunteer work, which will include painting and decorating, and which must first be approved by the Vestry or Executive Committee.

10. Establishes policy on pictures, signs, and items attached to walls in all areas of the building.

11. Ascertains security measures; sees that locks and lights are adequate. Keeps a master list of people with keys to church.

12. Ascertains that all local ordinances on such matters as fire extinguishers, garbage collections and sanitary codes are satisfactorily observed.

13. Maintains records for review of all purchases, suppliers and prices, as required.

14. Sets an example for the congregation in his public and private prayer life.

15. Delegates responsibilities appropriately while maintaining overall accountability for his function; recruits necessary personnel for effective performance.

Position: **FUND RAISING CHAIRMAN**

Reports to: **WARDEN AND ADMINISTRATIVE DE-
                     PARTMENT CHAIRMAN**

Function: **CO-ORDINATES ALL CHURCH WIDE
                     FUND RAISING ACTIVITIES**

Responsibilities:

1. In consultation with Rector and Wardens, appoints necessary personnel to manage individual fund raising events.

2. Receives and reviews all fund raising material sent to the church.

3. Attends necessary conferences in order to be informed about latest fund raising possibilities.

4. Schedules church fund raising events, in consultation with the Rector and Fellowship Chairman.

5. With the Membership Chairman, produces an annual directory of the congregation's membership, and includes paid advertisements from local businesses.

6. Plans and serves on capital funds campaigns as required.

7. Reports quarterly to the Vestry or Executive Committee on funds received and disbursed; also, requests annual budget to provide for fund raising expenses.

8. Sets an example for the congregation in his public and private prayer life.

9. Delegates responsibilities appropriately while maintaining overall accountability for his function; recruits necessary personnel for effective performance.

Position: **MEMORIALS AND BEQUESTS CHAIRMAN**

Reports to: **WARDEN AND ADMINISTRATIVE DE-PARTMENT CHAIRMAN**

Function: **CO-ORDINATES ALL GIFTS OF MONIES, FURNITURE, FURNISHINGS, AND EQUIP-MENT**

Responsibilities:

1. Maintains a record of all monies received for memorials, gifts of remembrance, and designated purposes.

2. Publishes annually a listing of gifts received, monies expended and funds accumulated during the previous twelve-month period. Traditionally, this report has been included in All Saints' Day services.

3. Investigates the capital needs of the church and secures estimated prices as a guide for donations.

4. Regularly publishes suggested gifts and their costs in the monthly newsletter. Also, keeps items of interest on bulletin boards current.

5. Establishes policies and procedures for proper recognition of donors, including installation of plaques and inscription in a Book of Memorials, which is to be prominently displayed.

6. Meets and discusses memorials with interested members, considering their wishes and suggestions.

7. Investigates potential sources of gifts outside the congregation and develops leads.

8. Appoints a custodian for a Book of Remembrance with the advice and consent of the Rector and Wardens. Also insures that proper publicity is given to the Book of Remembrance, which serves as a long-term endowment program based on small gifts from deaths, anniversaries, etc.

9. Assists the custodian of the Book of Remembrance in the establishment of policies and procedures, including a system for acknowledging gifts.

10. Assists Rector in educating congregation on matters

of deferred giving through wills, stocks, and insurance policies.

11. Sets an example for the congregation in his public and private prayer life.

12. Delegates responsibilities appropriately while maintaining overall accountability for his function; recruits necessary personnel for effective performance.

Position:	**PERSONNEL CHAIRMAN**
Reports to:	**WARDEN AND ADMINISTRATIVE DE-PARTMENT CHAIRMAN**
Function:	**MONITORS OVERALL INTERACTION OF VESTRY OR EXECUTIVE COMMITTEE AND ALL STAFF AS PER AGREED UPON WRITTEN STANDARDS**

Responsibilities:

1. Assists Rector and Wardens in defining staff requirements for the following:

a. salaried personnel

b. volunteer and part-time staff.

2. Assists all Chairmen in evaluating, reviewing, and updating position descriptions on an annual basis or as required.

3. Maintains a Rector's support group to monitor, the Rector's function and to be responsive to his and his family's needs.

4. Manages all contract negotiations with salaried personnel, with assistance from other members of the Vestry or Executive Committee as required. Also determines the following as applicable:

a. recommended fringe benefits, such as vacation time, sick pay, holidays

b. recommended compensation per hour, week, month, or year with payment schedule

c. definition of tenure and maximum length of service for all church functions

d. standards for evaluation and review.

5. Develops and maintains a data bank of membership interests and skills.

6. Insures that adequate records are maintained on all salaried personnel.

7. Reviews and provides for adequate insurance protection from fire, theft, liability, and workmen's compensation.

8. With the Rector, co-ordinates team effectiveness training events for the Vestry or Executive Committee, to be held as often as required, at least annually at a retreat and planning conference.

9. Provides regular feedback to the Vestry or Executive Committee on their team effectiveness, with special attention to group maintenance needs.

10. Participates in appropriate workshops and training events to insure effectiveness.

11. Sets an example for the congregation in his public and private prayer life.

12. Delegates responsibilities appropriately while maintaining overall accountability for his function; recruits necessary personnel for effective performance.

Position:	**SECRETARY OR CLERK**
Reports to:	**WARDEN AND ADMINISTRATIVE DE-PARTMENT CHAIRMAN**
Function:	**RECORDS AND MAINTAINS A WRITTEN RECORD OF ALL MEETINGS OF THE VESTRY OR EXECUTIVE COMMITTEE**

Responsibilities:

1. Insures a record of all meetings of the Vestry or Executive Committee in a brief, accurate and concise format.

2. Makes copies of minutes available no later than two weeks after the meeting at which they were taken.

3. Records all corrections, additions, and deletions accordingly.

4. Serves as custodian of all previous minutes and records. Also maintains a file of all written reports received by the Vestry or Executive Committee.

5. Serves as or appoints, with the Rector's and the Wardens' advice and consent, a Corresponding Secretary, who replies to all mail to the Vestry or Executive Committee within one week of receipt.

6. Serves as or appoints, with the Rector's and the Wardens' advice and consent, a Historian, who maintains all scrapbooks and other items of a lasting interest.

7. Introduces and reads as necessary all communications to the Vestry or Executive Committee.

8. Posts monthly minutes on bulletin board and makes copies available to membership of the congregation as required.

9. Sets an example for the congregation in his public and private prayer life.

10. Delegates responsibilities appropriately while maintaining overall accountability for his function; recruits necessary personnel for effective performance.

Position:	**STEWARDSHIP CHAIRMAN**
Reports to:	**WARDEN AND ADMINISTRATIVE DE-PARTMENT CHAIRMAN**
Function:	**DEVELOPS AND MAINTAINS A TOTAL YEAR ROUND PROGRAM AND EMPHASIS ON CHRISTIAN STEWARDSHIP FOR THE ENTIRE CONGREGATION**

Responsibilities:

1. Provides for an every member visitation program to be held at least once a year.

2. Organizes an ongoing financial stewardship program.

3. Serves as or appoints, with the advice and consent of the Rector and Wardens, an Every-Member-Canvass Chairman.

4. Introduces an overall orientation to Christian stewardship as a way of life, employing educational techniques and materials as required.

5. Secures necessary commitment from the leadership of the congregation to establish a stewardship standard for the members at large.

6. Encourages and supports participation of all members, especially youth and young adults.

7. Sees to it that all financial commitments are acknowledged promptly and that all commitments of time and talents are in fact utilized.

8. Assists in the development and implementation of an ongoing goal-identification and achievement program, for which good stewardship is required.

9. Participates in training events to enlarge and improve his capacity to function effectively. Also studies and reviews current materials on stewardship.

10. Sets an example for the congregation in his public and private prayer life.

11. Delegates responsibilities appropriately while maintaining overall accountability for his function; recruits necessary personnel for effective performance.

Position:	**CHRISTIAN EDUCATION CHAIRMAN**
Reports to:	**WARDEN AND PROGRAM DEPARTMENT CHAIRMAN**
Function:	**DEVELOPS AND MAINTAINS TOTAL ALL AGE CHRISTIAN EDUCATION PROGRAM FOR THE ENTIRE CONGREGATION**

Responsibilities:

1. In consultation with the Rector, co-ordinates all educational programs for youth and young people as follows:
 a. appoints a director for the church school
 b. assists in church school curriculum planning
 c. along with the director, insures church school teacher selection and training
 d. determines and secures necessary materials and supplies
 e. appoints leadership for young peoples' groups and assists in establishing program objectives.

2. In consultation with the Rector, co-ordinates all educational programs for adults as follows:
 a. provides for small study groups as required;
 b. develops family retreat program
 c. appoints tract-rack custodian to maintain current literature
 d. arranges for guest speakers as required
 e. encourages congregational participation in diocesan or area wide educational programs.

3. Works with the Stewardship Chairman in an ongoing goal-identification and achievement program.

4. Encourages and supports continuing education for clergy and consults with Rector as required on this matter.

5. Sets an example for the congregation in his public and private prayer life.

6. Delegates responsibilities appropriately while maintaining overall accountability for his function; recruits necessary personnel for effective performance.

Position: **COMMUNITY RELATIONS CHAIRMAN**

Reports to: **WARDEN AND PROGRAM DEPARTMENT CHAIRMAN**

Function: **CO-ORDINATES IMPACT OF THE CONGREGATION WITHIN THE OVERALL COMMUNITY**

Responsibilities:

1. Supervises all special outreach ministries and insures proper functioning, according to agreed upon policies and procedures, of the following:

    a. bus or transportation program for Sundays and/or weekdays

    b. community action in such areas as low income housing, public education, multiple zoning and planning, etc.

    c. day care program or young peoples' drop in center

    d. media ministry via radio and/or television, as well as newspaper publicity

    e. nursing home services

    f. outreach or "extra mile" projects

    g. senior citizens program, as well as shut-in visitation/communication program.

2. Insures that clear and adequate road signs direct people to the church.

3. Arranges for outside sign board to be properly maintained, and to include a listing of current services and events.

4. Provides for displays and bulletin board materials to emphasize needs beyond the local congregation

5. Annually recommends to the Vestry or Executive Committee a schedule for monthly special offering projects.

6. Assists the Rector in determining his appropriate participation within the life of the community.

7. Assists in development and maintenance of a local community blood drive.

8. Recommends to the Budget and Finance Committee an annual sum of money to be designated for the Rector's Discretionary Fund, after consultation with the Rector.

9. Sets an example for the congregation in his public and private prayer life.

10. Delegates responsibilities appropriately while maintaining overall accountability for his function; recruits necessary personnel for effective performance.

Position:	**ECUMENICAL RELATIONS CHAIRMAN**
Reports to:	**WARDEN AND PROGRAM DEPARTMENT CHAIRMAN**
Function:	**DEVELOPS PROGRAMS AND ACTIVITIES INVOLVING PEOPLE FROM OTHER DENOMINATIONS AND TRADITIONS ON BOTH FORMAL AND INFORMAL LEVELS**

Responsibilities:

1. Assists the Rector in his participation in the local ministerial association.

2. Participates in the local council of churches or association of congregations.

3. Represents the congregation at ecumenical events, as well as at significant activities in other congregations, such as the installation of a minister.

4. With the Evangelism Chairman, organizes distribution of a congregational directory, with an invitation to come and worship, to every member of the community.

5. Encourages and supports ecumenical educational programs, such as an Ecumenical Vacation Church School.

6. Encourages development of a sensitivity on the part of the congregation to the value and importance of ecumenical co-operation through discussions and participation in joint services.

7. Establishes formal covenant relationships with other congregations, with the approval of the Vestry or Executive Committee as necessary.

8. Assists Rector in securing supply clergy or in arranging joint services or pulpit exchanges.

9. Sets an example for the congregation in his public and private prayer life, attending worship services at other congregations in the community on a regular basis.

10. Delegates responsibilities appropriately while maintaining overall accountability for his function; recruits necessary personnel for effective performance.

Position:	**EVANGELISM CHAIRMAN**
Reports to:	**WARDEN AND PROGRAM DEPARTMENT CHAIRMAN**
Function:	**CO-ORDINATES AND TRAINS THE ENTIRE CONGREGATION TO BE WITNESSES FOR THE GOOD NEWS OF JESUS CHRIST**

Responsibilities:

1. Consults with other Chairmen to determine appropriate evangelistic emphases in their functions and responsibilities.

2. With the Rector, plans and produces spiritual encounters, through such programs as regular services of the Laying On of Hands and Faith-Alive Weekends.

3. Emphasizes pesonal behavior and commitment to the Lord Jesus as a model for people to follow.

4. With the Ecumenical Chairman, organizes distribution of a congregational directory, with an invitation to come and worship, to every member of the community.

5. Sets an example for the congregation in his public and private prayer life.

6. Delegates responsibilities appropriately while maintaining overall accountability for his function; recruits necessary personnel for effective performance.

Position:	**FELLOWSHIP CHAIRMAN**
Reports to:	**WARDEN AND PROGRAM DEPARTMENT CHAIRMAN**
Function:	**MAINTAINS COMMUNICATIONS AMONG ALL CHURCH ORGANIZATIONS AND DEVELOPS A CLOSE FELLOWSHIP AMONG THE ENTIRE CHURCH MEMBERSHIP**

Responsibilities:

1. Serves as a liaison between various church organizations and the Vestry or Executive Committee.

2. Chairs meetings of a parish council of church organizations, to co-ordinate activities as required.

3. Serves as or appoints, with the advice and consent of the Rector and Wardens, an Editor for the monthly newsletter.

4. With the Rector, maintains a schedule of all meetings, dates, times, and places; also posts meetings on a suitably located public parish calendar.

5. Develops natural groupings of people based on geographical proximity and similar hobbies and interests, such as a bridge or sewing club.

6. Promotes suppers, social events and trips in order to increase fellowship opportunities, as distinct from fund raising events.

7. Develops and maintains House Rules to apply to all persons utilizing church properties.

8. Sets an example for the congregation in his public and private prayer life.

9. Delegates responsibilities appropriately while maintaining overall accountability for his function; recruits necessary personnel for effective performance.

Position:	**MEMBERSHIP CHAIRMAN**
Reports to:	**WARDEN AND PROGRAM DEPARTMENT CHAIRMAN**
Function:	**SECURES AND ORIENTS NEW MEMBERS TO PARTICIPATE IN THE LIFE OF THE CONGREGATION**

Responsibilities:

1. Serves as or appoints a greeter (or greeters) to welcome newcomers at all services and public events held at the church.

2. Arranges periodic newcomers' receptions, to be held on at least a quarterly basis.

3. Obtains necessary information from new members for parish records, and encourages newcomers to request letters of transfer from their former congregations.

4. Maintains a file of newcomers' names along with church organization referrals and results.

5. With the Fund Raising Chairman produces an annual directory of the congregation's membership, and includes paid advertisements from local businesses.

6. Advises Rector as to suitability of a pastoral call on a newcomer.

7. Sets an example for the congregation in his public and private life.

8. Delegates responsibilities appropriately while maintaining overall accountability for his function; recruits necessary personnel for effective performance.

Position:	**WORSHIP CHAIRMAN**
Reports to:	**WARDEN AND PROGRAM DEPARTMENT CHAIRMAN**
Function:	**PROVIDES FOR NECESSARY PERSONNEL AND PROCEDURES TO INSURE ORDERLY AND WELL RUN WORSHIP SERVICES**

Responsibilities:

1. Serves as a listener and acts in an advisory capacity to the Rector with respect to concerns and needs of the congregation.

2. Under the canonical authority of the Rector, supervises all individuals and groups connected with worship services, including the following:

  a. Acolytes
  b. Altar Guild
  c. Choirs
  e. Lay Readers
  f. Ushers.

3. Assists in recruitment for above-named groups connected with worship services.

4. Oversees any necessary music consultation, including interviews for new organists and choirmasters, subject to the Rector's canonical authority.

5. In the absence of the Rector, provides supply clergy or other guest preachers and celebrants.

6. Insures that proper vestments are available for all participants in worship services.

7. Insures maintenance of inventory and supply of prayer and hymn books.

8. Provides for weekly delivery of flowers according to Rector's directions.

9. Assists Rector in establishing fee schedule for weddings, funerals, and other special services.

10. Acts as a spokesman for the various groups connected with worship services at the Vestry or Executive Committee.

11. Encourages and supports development of lay ministries through participation in appropriate workshops and conferences.

12. Sets an example for the congregation in his public and private prayer life.

13. Delegates responsibilities appropriately while maintaining overall accountability for his function; recruits necessary personnel for effective performance.

APPENDIX IV

Some Staff and Volunteer Position Descriptions

Position:	**CHURCH SECRETARY**
Reports to:	**RECTOR**
Function:	**PROVIDES NECESSARY ADMINISTRATIVE SUPPORT FOR THE RECTOR'S OFFICE**

Responsibilities:

1. Performs all secretarial duties as directed by the Rector.

2. Types and duplicates all correspondance, mailings and reports as required.

3. Serves as a public relations contact and assists in direct inquiries to appropriate sources.

4. Maintains all files with current material as directed by the Rector.

5. Oversees operations and maintenance of all office equipment.

6. Maintains inventory of supplies and purchases necessary items as per office and printing and bulletins budget.

7. Maintains and administers petty cash and stamp account as per budget requirements.

8. Answers telephone, provides coverage when office is unattended and insures appropriate attention to inquiries.

9. Maintains parish records on all baptisms, marriages, deaths, transfers, and confirmations.

10. Keeps such statistical data as may be required, under the direction of the Rector.

11. Opens all mail, except personally addressed correspondence, and promptly routes contents to appropriate personnel.

12. Maintains message slots for all organizations and leaders in the church.

13. Reviews terms of employment on an annual basis with the Rector and personnel committee members as required.

14. Responds to all church business in a confidential manner.

15. If a member of the congregation, sets an example in public and private prayer life.

Position:	**BOOKKEEPER-ACCOUNTANT**
Reports to:	**TREASURER**
Function:	**PROVIDES NECESSARY SUPPORT IN FISCAL MATTERS FOR THE OFFICE OF THE TREASURER**

Responsibilities:

1. Maintains accurate financial records of receipts and disbursements, as directed by the Treasurer in conjunction with the budget and finance committee.

2. Makes all deposits on banking day immediately following receipt and insures proper security of all monies, as directed by the Treasurer.

3. Checks that all dividends and interest payments from investments are received and properly noted.

4. Maintains necessary records on all bequests and designated monies.

5. Audits all accounts payable, ascertaining proper receipt of all goods and services, and prepares voucher checks for Treasurer's review and signature.

6. Maintains current expenditure file and draws all checks promptly or as funds are available.

7. Administers depreciation schedule on all furniture and equipment.

8. Insures proper bidding procedure for all major repairs, replacements, and additions.

9. Prepares all financial reports, at the direction of the Treasurer.

10. Supervises petty cash fund and stamp account maintained by the Church Secretary.

11. Serves as custodian of financial records and determines schedule of retention and destruction of all church fiscal papers.

12. Performs such other duties as may be assigned by the Treasurer.

13. Reviews terms of employment on an annual basis with the Treasurer and personnel committee members as required.

14. Responds to all church business in a confidential manner.

15. If a member of the congregation, sets an example in public and private prayer life.

Position: **CUSTODIAN/JANITOR/SEXTON**

Reports to: **RECTOR AND/OR CHAIRMAN BUILD-
                 INGS AND GROUNDS**

Function: **PROVIDES NECESSARY MAINTENANCE
                 OF BUILDINGS AND GROUNDS AS RE-
                 QUIRED**

Responsibilities:

1. Cleans designated areas to be free of dust, dirt and spots, according to a written schedule agreed upon by the buildings and grounds committee.

2. Keeps all approaches and passageways free of debris, and ascertains safety of these areas.

3. Insures that all appropriate outside areas are promptly cleared of all snow and ice.

4. Maintains lawns and shrubbery as required by the buildings and grounds committee.

5. Maintains all electrical fixtures and furniture, making repairs as directed by the buildings and grounds committee.

6. Reports regularly to the Rector for co-ordination of arrangements for use of church facilities.

7. Sets up chairs, tables, and other equipment for meetings, as required and directed by the Rector.

8. Insures proper operation of heating and cooling systems.

9. Insures opening and closing of church according to written schedule, and inspects security of locks and windows.

10. Assists at special services and regularly scheduled services as required.

11. Performs such other duties as may be assigned by the Rector or the chairman of the buildings and grounds committee.

12. Reviews terms of employment on an annual basis with the chairman of the buildings and grounds committee and personnel committee members as required.

13. Responds to all church business in a confidential manner.

14. If a member of the congregation, sets an example in public and private prayer life.

Position: **ORGANIST AND CHOIRMASTER**

Reports to: **RECTOR**

Function: **PROVIDES FOR THE CHURCH'S TOTAL MUSICAL REQUIREMENTS UNDER THE AUTHORITY OF THE RECTOR**

Responsibilities:

1. Serves as a liturgical consultant to the Rector in preparation and performance of all services.

2. Serves as a member of the worship committee *ex officio*.

3. Selects hymns and choral pieces as required by the Rector.

4. Recruits and trains choir with weekly rehearsals.

5. Maintains all musical equipment and supplies as required.

6. Maintains appropriate musical library according to annually approved music budget.

7. Develops and maintains a fee schedule for music at special services.

8. Provides for maintenance of all choir vestments, to include cleaning, repairs and a current inventory record.

9. Plays the organ at all regularly scheduled services and secures a substitute organist as required.

10. Offers a variety of musical settings and instruments, when appropriate, in order to enrich the quality of worship through music.

11. Performs such other duties as may be assigned by the Rector.

12. Reviews terms of employment on an annual basis with the Rector and the chairman of the worship committee, as well as members of the personnel committee as required.

13. Responds to all church business in a confidential manner.

14. If a member of the congregation, sets an example in public and private prayer life.

Position:	**ACOLYTE/CRUCIFER/SERVER**
Reports to:	**RECTOR**
Function:	**ASSISTS AT THE ALTAR DURING SERVICES AS REQUIRED AND DIRECTED BY THE RECTOR**

Responsibilities:

1. Performs duties as trained, under procedures approved by the Rector.

2. Conforms to broad dress standards of dark shoes and white or light colored shirt as approved by the Rector.

3. Maintains vestments assigned by the supervisor of acolytes and brings needed repairs to his or her attention.

4. Serves at the altar as scheduled and arranges for substitute when unable to participate.

5. Checks with officiating minister before the start of a service to receive any special instructions.

6. Conducts him or her self in an appropriate manner, while serving and in everyday life.

7. Attends meetings of the acolytes and training sessions, unless excused by the Rector.

8. Sets an example for the congregation in public and private prayer life.

Position: **ALTAR GUILD DIRECTOR**

Reports to: **RECTOR**

Function: **CO-ORDINATES PLACEMENT OF ALL ALTAR FURNISHINGS, FABRIC, AND SUPPLIES FOR ALL SERVICES**

Responsibilities:

1. Consults with the Rector on a regular basis to insure altar appointments are appropriate for all services.

2. Serves as presiding officer of the altar guild, according to guild's bylaws.

3. Recruits and trains new members as required.

4. Maintains inventory of all altar supplies and orders replacements as budgeted.

5. Schedules altar guild members to prepare and clear altar for all services.

6. Develops and maintains standard operating procedures, with the Rector's advice and consent.

7. Insures cleanliness and good repair of all altar fabric and vestments.

8. Maintains a flower chart and solicits participation from the congregation on an annual basis or as required.

9. Sets an example for the congregation in public and private prayer life.

Position: **CHURCH SCHOOL DIRECTOR OR
                   SUPERINTENDENT**

Reports to: **CHRISTIAN EDUCATION CHAIRMAN**

Function: **SUPERVISES OVERALL CHURCH SCHOOL
                   PROGRAM ACCORDING TO CHRISTIAN
                   EDUCATION COMMITTEE POLICIES**

Responsibilities:

1. Appoints necessary teachers and staff, in consultation with the Rector as required.

2. Co-ordinates all church school activities and programs.

3. Insures adequate inventory of supplies and materials for all classes, operating on an annually approved budget.

4. Recommends curiculum for approval by the Christian education committee.

5. Provides teacher training and meetings on a regular basis.

6. Prepares reports and an annual church school information booklet, as required.

7. Sets an example for staff, teachers, students, and the congregation in both public and private prayer life.

Position:	**CHIEF LAY READER**
Reports to:	**RECTOR**
Function:	**PROVIDES LAY PARTICIPATION IN SERVICES AS DIRECTED BY THE RECTOR**

Responsibilities:

1. Consults with the Rector on a regular basis to insure reader participation at services as required.

2. Serves as presiding officer of lay readers according to their bylaws.

3. Trains and schedules lay readers, according to written standards approved by the Rector.

4. Encourages and supports lay reader workshops and conferences.

5. Recruits members as required, according to Canon 25.

6. Performs such other duties as may be assigned from time to time by the Rector.

7. Conducts him or her self in an appropriate manner, while reading and in every day life.

8. Sets an example for the congregation in public and private prayer life.

Position: **HEAD USHER**

Reports to: **RECTOR AND WORSHIP COMMITTEE CHAIRMAN**

Function: **PROVIDES FOR A GRACIOUS AND OR-DERLY MOVEMENT OF PEOPLE, BEFORE, DURING, AND AFTER ALL SERVICES**

Responsibilities:

1. Consults with Rector on a regular basis to insure that ushers are at all services.

2. Serves as presiding officer at meetings of the ushers, to be held at least semi-annually.

3. Trains and schedules ushers according to written stand-ards approved by the Rector and the worship committee.

4. Insures that Bibles, hymnals, prayer books, and bulle-tins, are provided at services as required.

5. Keeps all books used at services in good condition and notifies worship committee promptly when replacements are necessary.

6. Confirms attendance and number of communions at all public services.

7. Recruits ushers as required and performs such other duties as may be assigned from time to time by the Rector.

8. Conducts him or her self in an appropriate manner, while ushering and in every day life.

9. Sets an example for the congregation in public and private prayer life.

BIBLIOGRAPHY

Crockett, W. David. *Promotion and Publicity for Churches.* New York: Morehouse-Barlow Co., Inc., 1974.

————. *Sound Financial Stewardship.* New York: Morehouse-Barlow Co., Inc., 1973.

Dawley, Powel Mills. *Chapters in Church History*, rev. ed. Greenwich, Connecticut: The Seabury Press, 1963.

Diggs, Dorothy C. *A Working Manual for Altar Guilds*, 2d ed. New York: Morehouse-Barlow Co., Inc., 1968.

Drucker, Peter F. *The Effective Executive.* New York: Harper & Row, Publishers, 1966.

Fenn, Don Frank. *Parish Administration.* New York: Morehouse-Gorham Co., Inc., 1951.

Hersey, Paul and Blanchard, Kenneth H. *Management of Organizational Behavior.* Englewood Cliffs, New Jersey: Prentice-Hall, Inc., 1969.

Lawrence, William Appleton. *Parsons, Vestries, and Parishes.* Greenwich, Connecticut: The Seabury Press, 1961.

Rudge, Peter F. *Ministry and Management.* London, England: Tavistock Publications, 1968.

Stewart, Alexander D. *The Clergyman as Administrator.* Unpublished M.B.A. Thesis, Graduate School of Business, Harvard, 1961.

NOTES

NOTES

NOTES